MASTERING
LIFE
BEFORE IT'S TOO LATE

10 Biblical Strategies for a Lifetime of Purpose

Robert J. Morgan

HOWARD BOOKS
An Imprint of Simon & Schuster, Inc.
New York   Nashville   London   Toronto   Sydney   New Delhi

Howard Books
An Imprint of Simon & Schuster, Inc.
1230 Avenue of the Americas
New York, NY 10020

To Owen

CONTENTS

THE FOURTH PATTERN
Maximize the Morning

THE FIFTH PATTERN
Pull Off at Rest Stops

THE SIXTH PATTERN
Operate on Yourself

THE SEVENTH PATTERN
Live As If

THE EIGHTH PATTERN
Bathe in the Dead Sea

THE NINTH PATTERN
Practice the Power of Plodding

THE TENTH PATTERN
Remember There Are Two of You

I love to think that God appoints
My portion day by day;
Events of life are in His hand,
And I would only say,
Appoint them in Thine own good time,
And in Thine own best way.

—Anna Waring [1]

Mastering Life the Master's Way

If we could sit down together for a cup of coffee, this is what I'd like to tell you. We have a limited number of days on earth, and we don't know how many are left. We believe we're on this planet for a reason, but most people can't figure out what it is. Our ability to influence the world is directly proportional to our knack for managing our own lives, but we have trouble with that too. We search everywhere for ways to improve, yet the only truly effective life is one unapologetically woven from the strands of Scripture.

That's what this book is about. Over the decades, and from a lifetime of Bible study, I've extrapolated ten lessons that have made all the difference to me. I've tested them in the tumblers of time. These are lifelong rhythms for lifetime usefulness—the godly patterns of productive souls. These truths are as dear to me as friends. They may or may not seem profound to you—there's an undeniable simplicity about them. But these are the instructions I want to pass along to my children and grandchildren, and to you.

They're embedded in the Bible like veins of gold, and it's hard to discover them elsewhere, though we often pan in other creeks. Through the years, for example, I've read more nonfiction books than I can recall, and in many fields: biography, business, history, philosophy, leadership, management, personal development, positive thinking, inspiration, self-help, and so forth. I've gleaned something from most of them, but, with rare exceptions, they've missed the essential element. To master life, we must know the Master Himself and gain mastery of His Word.

The Bible is the best self-improvement course ever devised. According to Scripture, our days are not accidental or incidental. We are not random or rudderless souls. We have a heavenly Father who orders our steps and ordains our stops; who ordains our times and assigns our tasks; who equips us to do His will and to work in us what is pleasing to Him.

This means the Lord has designed a wonderful life, tailor-made to our exact specifications. "We are God's handiwork," said the apostle Paul, "created in Christ Jesus to do good works, which God prepared in advance for us to do" (Ephesians 2:10). The Savior thinks of us the way an artist plans a painting; a potter molds a vessel; a sculptor forms a statue; a weaver produces a beautiful tapestry. We are His works in progress.

Your personality is yours alone. Your calling and gifts are unique; your background is singular; your legacy can be achieved by no one else on earth. There's a special blueprint for your life, with no other name on the page. Your strengths, struggles, and situations are not hit-or-miss. All your days are designed in advance before any of them appears on the calendar, and God longs to fulfill His plan in your life just as fully as His will is done in heaven.

This reality changes everything. We know it's true because it's taught on every page of Scripture. The Bible says,

> His divine power has given us everything we need for a godly life through our knowledge of him who called us by his own glory and goodness. Through these he has given us his very great and precious promises, so that through them you may participate in the divine nature, having escaped the corruption in the world caused by evil desires. For this very reason, make every effort to add to your faith goodness . . .

knowledge . . . self-control . . . perseverance . . . godliness . . .
mutual affection and . . . love. For if you possess these qualities in increasing measure, they will keep you from being
ineffective and unproductive. (2 Peter 1:3–8)

You can begin living this way now. His divine power has given everything you need. His precious promises open the door to endless
resources. You can possess the qualities of Christ Himself in increasing measure and learn to be pleasant and productive by His grace
and glory. The habits I'll describe are the primary colors God uses in
painting this kind of life.

These ten patterns for pleasantly productive people can be implemented today whether you're a student or a senior adult, whether
a novice or an executive. These principles can be taught to children,
and they can be learned by leaders. They're strong enough to change
us from within, practical enough to make us purposeful and productive, and durable enough to keep us cheerful and positive. Whatever
your age or stage in life, there's no reason to waste another day, no
excuse for squandering a life by failing to finish the mission assigned
to us by the Lord Jesus.

- Jesus said, "My food is to do the will of him who sent
  me and to finish his work." (John 4:34)

- Before returning to heaven, He told His disciples He
  was leaving "each with their assigned task." (Mark
  13:34)

- The apostle Paul said, "Life is worth nothing to me
  unless I use it for finishing the work assigned me by
  the Lord Jesus." (Acts 20:24)[2]

- Paul told the Corinthians, "What, after all, is Apollos?

And what is Paul? Only servants . . . as the Lord has
assigned to each his task." (1 Corinthians 4:5)

• Colossians 4:17 says, "See to it that you complete the
work you have received in the Lord."³

Success is doing the will of God and doing it with the right attitudes
and in one-day increments as He assigns the work—being synchronized with the sacred. This is what the apostle Paul meant when he
said, "I can do all things through him who gives me strength" (Philippians 4:13). In other words, "I can do everything God assigns
me today, through Him who infuses me with the needed strength.
I can be pleasantly productive in fulfilling God's will for my life this
day." If we master life in the Master's way, the accumulation of our
days will produce a legacy planned in heaven that unfolds on earth
during the exact span of our lives, down to the last hour. Otherwise
we'll spin through our days bewildered by the busyness and brevity
of them all.

When I was a boy, my buddy and I used to sneak into my
mother's laundry corner in the basement and climb inside her dry-
ing machine to take turns tumbling around on the fluff cycle. Evidently in those days manufacturers didn't devise many safety
mechanisms, so we had loads of fun tossing around like dish-
cloths. Though never caught, we were eventually hampered by
size. We grew too big for the drum and had to throw in the towel.

All these years later, I sometimes feel I'm still spinning around
like a rag in hot air or stuck on permanent press. Without a sense of
God's ordaining control over my hours and days, I'd be lost in the
whirlpool. But if I take things in day-size installments and operate in
the strength He provides, using my moments wisely, I can do my
best, leave the undone with the Lord, and let Him take care of the
results. Maybe it's time for you, too, to move from the spin cycle to

the grace cycle, get life sorted out, iron out the wrinkles, find and finish your assigned purposes, and master life before it's too late.

In a letter dated April 29, 1519, Swiss Reformer Ulrich Zwingli wrote these words to one of his heroes, Dutch scholar Desiderius Erasmus: "It was that spirited energy of yours I was in search of. It was the courtesy of your character and your well-regulated life that I admired."[4]

That's what we all need—spirited energy, courtesy, character, and a well-regulated life. We need to start each morning zealous to complete God's agenda for the present day. Nothing compares to being about our Father's business. Nothing is more important than making each day and every moment count. If you're ready to move from the spin cycle of life to the grace cycle and to have a life of spirited energy, you'll find a workable plan in the upcoming chapters. We'll talk about getting ourselves organized, starting each day on the right note, and tending to our rest and to our souls. We'll also explore living by faith, cultivating inner joy, and doing what God has assigned and no more. Finally, we'll talk about persevering in our assigned duties to the end, and letting the Holy Spirit relive the life of Jesus through us. In a nutshell, this is the formula for mastering life. These are the truths you'll find in the following chapters. When we abide in Christ like a branch in a vine, we'll produce a vintage life.

Thus with cheerfulness shall we reap the fruit of a
well-informed mind and a well-regulated life.

—Hymnist Philip Doddridge on the effect
of Scripture-based self-improvement[5]

Thank you for picking up this book. Please read it, highlight sentences that speak to you, copy key thoughts onto cards for posting, persist in developing the suggested habits, and pass along nuggets that are helpful to you. For further help and group interaction, check out our free downloadable *Mastering Life Before It's Too Late* workbook at www.robertjmorgan.com.

My prayer for you is one from Hebrews 13:20–21, a benediction I often repeat to my church at the end of our worship services at The Donelson Fellowship in Nashville:

> *Now may the God of peace,*
> *who through the blood of the eternal covenant*
> *brought back from the dead our Lord Jesus,*
> *that great Shepherd of the sheep,*
> *equip you with everything good for doing his will,*
> *and may he work in us what is pleasing to him,*
> *through Jesus Christ,*
> *to whom be glory for ever and ever.*
> *Amen.*

THE FIRST PATTERN

Listen to a Twelve-Year-Old

Our main business is not to see
what lies dimly at a distance,
but to do what lies clearly at hand.

—Thomas Carlyle[1]

First Words, Last Words—Our Stencil for Success

One afternoon when my three daughters were younger—this happened in May of 1987—I came home after work and asked my wife, Katrina, how they had gotten along at school. "Oh, fine," she said. "Today was field day so they didn't have classes. They had games and competitions outside."

"How did they do?"

"None of the girls won first place," said Katrina. "But Victoria came home with three ribbons. Hannah won a ribbon too, I think, but she lost it on the way home. She's in her room."

Hannah, the middle child and in the second grade, was always a special focus of fatherly concern, so I went to her room to find her playing on the floor with her dolls and toys. I lay down on the carpet and asked her how her day had gone. She answered as usual: "Fine."

"It was field day, wasn't it?" I asked.

"Yeah."

"How did you do?"

"Okay, I guess."

There was a long pause, and I thought of my childhood experiences with field day. I was nonathletic, so sporting events were dreaded affairs. Thinking the same might be true for Hannah, I wanted to encourage her. "Hannah," I said, "we had field day when I was a boy, but I never did very well."

"You didn't?"

"No. It was terrible. I wasn't good at sports. I was always the last one chosen for teams. The best players would select who they wanted on their teams, and I was always the last one."

Another pause.

"It was humiliating."

Another pause.

"And whatever team I was on always lost. In fact, I don't remember ever being in a ball game of any kind in which my team won. And if we did win, it was in spite of me. I couldn't catch or throw or hit or anything. I just wasn't coordinated."

I continued dolefully along these lines for a few moments, and finally Hannah looked up from her toys and interrupted me. "Well, Dad," she said sympathetically, "sometimes you have to put your childhood behind you and get on with the rest of your life."

There was nothing to say after that except, "Well, yes, of course you're right. Thank you, Hannah. I love you."

"I love you too, Dad. Good-bye."

We occasionally learn more from our children than they learn from us. Every schoolteacher knows that the wisdom of the ages sometimes rolls off small tongues. As the psalmist said, God often speaks from the mouths of babes.[2]

A number of precocious children show up in the pages of the Bible, but one example outshines them all. There once was a boy who, at age twelve, spoke a sentence so simple in its wisdom and perception that it has the power to transform the way we wake up every morning and retire every evening. No child ever spoke as this one did, and His first documented sentence is a veritable motto for life. The first recorded words of the boy Jesus provide the first lesson in becoming a pleasantly productive person.

All the statements of Christ are priceless, of course, and His sermons in the Gospels represent the greatest body of enriching material ever assembled. No one ever spoke as He did. His Sermon on the Mount has been studied and practiced for two millennia. His command to be "born again" has transformed more people than any mandate ever spoken. His seven last words on the cross have been dissected by sixty generations. His Golden Rule is the baseline for all ethical conduct.

I have a Bible in which all the statements of Jesus are printed in red. Last year I sat down, starting with Matthew, and read through the four Gospels, skipping everything except the red letters. Somehow it changed the way I viewed Jesus and the accounts of His ministry. The plain words of Christ are succinct, powerful, and capable of altering our lives in a single reading. It was a bracing spiritual exercise, one I recommend.

Chronologically, this red thread begins with a couple of sentences spoken before Jesus was even a teenager. Of the four Gospel writers, only Luke records much about the first thirty years of our Lord's life, telling us about the birth of Jesus and about what happened to Him when He was eight days old, forty days old, twelve years old, and thirty years old. These specific events are linked with one-sentence summaries covering the intervening years.

According to the stated purpose at the beginning of his Gospel, Luke based his Christ biography on eyewitness testimony. He carefully investigated everything from the beginning so he could write an orderly account, that we "may know the certainty of the things" we have been taught (see Luke 1:1–4). I believe much of the content of Luke 1 and 2 came from Luke's personal interviews with the virgin Mary, probably in her home in Ephesus in the mid-first century: the announcements by the angel Gabriel, Mary's visit to Elizabeth, the birth of John the Baptist, the trek from Nazareth to Bethlehem, the birth of Christ, the angels over Shepherds' Field, and the Nativity stories of old Simeon and aged Anna in the temple. I imagine Mary related quite a bit of information about the childhood and upbringing of Jesus, but the Holy Spirit prompted

Luke to record only one story from our Lord's middle-childhood years.

Here's the remarkable account: "Every year Jesus' parents went to Jerusalem for the Festival of the Passover. When he was twelve years old, they went up to the festival, according to the custom. After the festival was over, while his parents were returning home, the boy Jesus stayed behind in Jerusalem, but they were unaware of it" (Luke 2:41–43).

Perhaps Jesus simply overslept that morning, but I think there's more to it. We have the impression the boy deliberately stayed behind in Jerusalem, knowing full well everyone had left without Him. Because friends and family traveled en masse to the Jewish feasts and because Jesus was a responsible lad who could look out for Himself, Joseph and Mary apparently didn't conduct a head count. They simply assumed Jesus was with His buddies or other family members.

"Thinking he was in their company, they traveled on for a day. Then they began looking for him among their relatives and friends. When they did not find him, they went back to Jerusalem to look for him" (Luke 2:44–45). Any parent can understand the panic that seized Joseph and Mary. I once lost one of my girls in a department store. She had wandered into an adjacent aisle, but for about a minute I was in full panic mode.

For Mary, the memories of those days must have been as vivid as when they occurred. Her preteen had disappeared in one of the most turbulent cities on earth and was missing three days while she and Joseph desperately searched for Him. Think of it! Joseph and Mary were entrusted to raise the Son of God—and they'd misplaced Him!

We can only imagine the waves of relief that swept over them when they finally saw their son sitting unperturbed in the temple, holding court with the Jewish theologians. Mary, whose exasperation mirrored her relief, said, "Son, why have you done this to us? You father and I have been frantic, searching for you everywhere."[3]

That occasioned our Lord's first known statement, recorded in Luke 2:49: "Why did you seek Me?" He asked. "Did you not know that I must be about My Father's business?"[4]

The Bible gives us this story, not only because it dominated Mary's memories of our Lord's childhood, but also because it was remarkably prophetic. Twenty-one years later, the same man— Jesus—would be in the same city—Jerusalem—at the same time— the Passover. He would again disappear from sight, triggering unspeakable anguish in Mary and among His friends. The duration would be exactly the same—three days. Then He would be suddenly reunited with His friends amid indescribable relief and great astonishment. The rationale for both events was the same: He had to be about His Father's business.[5]

There was nothing accidental about our twelve-year-old Lord's adventure. It was a prophetic preview. Whether Jesus in His childhood humanity understood all the ramifications of His words is an open question. As a boy of twelve, did He realize His destiny at Calvary? Was He yearning for information about the Messiah from the temple rabbis, being drawn to that subject like iron to magnet? We don't know; the answers to those questions reside in the realm of mystery. But there's no doubt He understood that however His life unfolded, He had to be about His Father's business. From His earliest impulses, Jesus was drawn toward a purposeful commitment to obey the will of God and to fulfill His mission, whatever it was. He knew His life had meaning. He knew an agenda had been wisely established for His days. He knew the Father had a purpose and a plan, and He wanted His soul to be acclimatized to His Father's prognostications. Otherwise, His brief time on earth would be wasted and worthless.

If those were the first recorded words of our Lord's earthly life, what were His last? John 19:30 provides the answer by taking us to the foot of the cross of Calvary: "When he had received the drink, Jesus said, 'It is finished.' With that, he bowed his head and gave up his spirit." He had completed His Father's business and finished the work of providing redemption for the world.

When I frame these two scenes and hang them on the walls of my mind, I'm staggered at the contrast. The first painting shows a perceptive boy with a clear, inquisitive face, fully engaged in conversations with His elders, curious about His future, excited about His Father's business. The other pictures a tortured victim, body streaked with blood, face burning in agony, parched lips whispering in painful gasps, "It is finished!"

Our Lord's dying words were not random. The previous evening, Jesus had expressed the same thought while offering His high priestly prayer to the Father, as recorded in John 17. In verse 4, Jesus prayed: "I have brought you glory on earth by finishing the work you gave me to do." This implies that Jesus assumed His life had purpose, that His work was pre-planned and pre-assigned, that He was on a divine timetable, and that the mission was being completed in a way that glorified the Father.

These two sentences—"I must be about My Father's business" and "I have brought you glory on earth by finishing the work you gave me to do"—are the verbal bookends of the life of Jesus Christ, and they serve as our template, model, mold, and standard in life.

If we're going to master life and fulfill the distinctive purpose God has for us, we have to say: "There are many things I can do in life, I have many possible venues and avenues, many options and opportunities, many decisions and distractions. But Christ gave me a pattern to follow, and He died to provide eternal life. Under His lordship, I pledge to live for Him, to devote myself to the Father's business from this moment and forever. I want to find and fulfill

God's unique docket and destiny for my life, whatever it means—just like Jesus."

"My food," said Jesus in John 4:34, "is to do the will of him who sent me and to finish his work." Pause a moment to say these words aloud and see if they ring true for you: "My food is to do the will of Him who sent Me and to finish His work."

As followers of Christ, we have inherited the Family Business, so to speak. We're partners with Christ in His Father's business, created to accomplish a set of purposes that God has established in advance for us to do. This doesn't mean everyone needs to earn their paycheck from a ministry organization. It's not really a matter of being a pastor or missionary or someone who is vocationally set aside and financially supported by a church-related group. It means we start living for Christ with all our hearts today, wherever we are, looking around to see what we can do for Him. Near you today is a need to fill. Close at hand is a person to cheer. Throughout the day you'll find tasks only you can tackle, and they represent the "food" of doing the will of the One who sent us.

A young man who visited me last week was troubled about working for the phone company, when he had prepared all his life for "ministry." He liked his job, but his family and friends nagged him about finding a job somewhere on a church staff.

"If the Lord leads you to a church staff, that's great," I told him, "but don't worry about it. Right now the phone company has hired you to be a minister on their staff, and they're paying your ministerial salary. They don't see it that way, but that's the reality. You are surrounded all day by customers and employees who need a smile, a bit of hope, an encouraging word, wise counsel, and the witness of a godly life. As time goes by, you'll find ways of sharing your faith. You can reach people no one else will see. You're in full-time ministry, assigned to the phone company, and the church isn't encumbered with your ministerial salary."

Yes, God is sovereign. Yes, we do have a certain freedom of the will. No one understands how God's sovereign will for our lives intersects with our ability to choose our path. Though our lives are pre-planned, it doesn't mean we have no choices. We have a full range of choices, for we can choose or reject God's agenda.

The decision to adopt God's will for yourself is a lifetime, life-long choice, and it's the only true starting place for mastering life. The apostle Paul summed it up with these words:

> Therefore, I urge you, brothers and sisters, in view of God's mercy, to offer your bodies a living sacrifice, holy and pleasing to God—this is your true and proper worship. Do not conform to the pattern of this world, but be transformed by the renewing of your mind. Then you will be able to test and approve what God's will is—his good, pleasing, and perfect will. (Romans 12:1–2)

On the basis of God's mercy and Christ's cross, you can determine now, at this moment, to offer yourself as a living sacrifice, transformed, living out God's will and determined to be pleasantly productive for Him during your remaining minutes, days, and years on earth.

It's as simple as saying, "Yes, Lord!"

Keep Thou my feet;
I do not ask to see
The distant scene;
One step enough for me.

—John Henry Newman[1]

2

Just for Today

O ur Father's business may consume our lifetimes, but we can't just think of it in lifelong terms. Having made an abiding decision to commit ourselves to the lordship of Christ and the will of God, we must then reduce it to bite-size realities, which we call "days." With the trajectory of our lives aligned Godward, we can faithfully implement this attitude on a daily basis. Awakening each morning, we can say: "This is the day the Lord has made for me. Today I must be about His business." We can offer the prayer Paul uttered in Acts 22:10: "Lord, what do you want me to do?"[2] We can say as the old soldier did every morning during his crack-of-dawn devotions: "Your assignment today, Sir!" The unfolding day then no longer belongs to us; we become servants and stewards of the minutes and moments God has ordained for us.

Elizabeth Fry is remembered as the "Angel of Prisons" because of her incessant efforts at prison reform in nineteenth-century England. She was the driving force behind laws making prisons more humane, and today her likeness adorns the Bank of England's five-pound note. Behind her reformer's zeal was an abiding desire to wake up every morning to serve the Lord. Before she passed away at age sixty-five, Elizabeth affirmed that she had never awakened from sleep, whether in sickness or in health, without her first waking thought being "How best may I serve my Lord?"[3]

When we begin the day in a similar way, we can close the day more fittingly. At the end of the evening, our work behind us, we can tuck ourselves into bed with the terminal words of Christ echoing in our evening prayers: "It is finished for today. I have brought You glory this day by finishing the work You assigned, as best I could." Our to-do lists may be longer at the end of the day than at the beginning, and we may feel we left much undone. But if we committed the day to the Lord, doing our best to accomplish His will during the intervening hours, we can leave both the done and the undone in His hands and fall asleep with a sense of completion and contentment.

If we sincerely before the Lord plan out our day along the lines suggested and carry it out to the best of our ability, we can and must leave it there. We should refuse to get into the bondage about what has not been done.

—J. Oswald Sanders[4]

Anna Warner, the author of the children's hymn "Jesus Loves Me," wrote a poem about this, which also became a popular hymn in its day:

> One more day's work for Jesus,
> One less of life for me!
> But Heaven is nearer and Christ is clearer
> Than yesterday to me.
> His love and light fill all my soul tonight.[5]

The second verse begins: "One more day's work for Jesus! / How sweet the work has been." And the poem ends with these prayerful words: "Lord, if I may, I'll serve another day!"[6]

In his book of hymn stories, the great song leader Ira Sankey wrote of a washerwoman who, while passing a mission chapel, heard a group of children singing this song. She was struck with the words, and she pondered them the next day as she bent over her washtub. *Have I ever done one day's work for Jesus in all my life?* she asked herself. That marked a turning point for her. Then and there she began doing her work each day for the Lord. She washed clothes for Jesus, cleaned the house for Jesus, took care of her family for Jesus. She began practicing Colossians 3:23: "Whatever you do, work at it with all your heart, as working for the Lord, not for human masters." According to Sankey, "A new light came into her life; and at the close of that day she could sing with a different feeling and new enthusiasm: 'One more day's work for Jesus! How sweet the work has been.'"[7]

We're not all washerwomen, but many of us toil away at tasks seldom noticed by others. We're not always doing great things, but anything done in the spirit of Colossians 3:23 is great in God's sight. The smallest duty, if Christ assigns it and we accomplish it, is grander in God's eyes than building the pyramids or acquiring a vast domain. After we've undertaken each day's work for Jesus, we can lay our heads on our pillows night after night, knowing we've been about our Father's business. The next morning we arise to a new God-planned day, and we find joy in the journey. Every day is a divine adventure.

When we consistently adopt this mind-set as a sustained, thanks-filled pattern, the days will fold into the weeks, and the weeks into the years, the years into the decades—and that's what we call faithfulness. Faithfulness isn't defined by a solitary act or achieved in a single day; it's a long obedience in the same direction, to borrow Eugene Peterson's phrase.[8] But if we string together our days of faithfulness like small jewels on a golden chain, we'll arrive at the end of our earthly span to present the treasure to the Lord and exchange it for a crown. We can say, "I have brought You glory on earth by finishing the work You gave me to do. It is finished." His response will be, "Well done, good and faithful servant."

Whenever I read the works of J. C. Ryle, a nineteenth-century Anglican bishop from Liverpool, I come away informed, inspired, or both. Here are his stirring words about the zeal of living a life devoted to "one thing":

> Zeal in Christianity is a burning desire to please God, to do his will, and to advance his glory in the world in every possible way. This desire is so strong when it really reigns in a person it impels them to make any sacrifice, to go through any trouble, to deny themselves anything, to suffer, to work, to labor, to toil, to spend themselves and be spent, and even to die, if only they can please God and honor Christ.
>
> A zealous person in Christianity is preeminently a person of one thing. It is not enough to say they are earnest, strong, uncompromising, meticulous, wholehearted, and fervent in spirit. They only see one thing, they care for one thing, they live for one thing, they are swallowed up in one thing; and that one thing is to please God. Whether they live or die, whether they are healthy or sick, whether they are rich or poor, whether they please man or give offense, whether they are thought wise or foolish, whether they are accused or praised—for all this the zealous person cares nothing at all.
>
> They have a passion for one thing, and that one thing is to please God and to advance God's glory. If they are consumed in the very burning of their passion for God, they don't care; they are content. They feel that, like a candle, they were made to burn; and if they are consumed in the burning, then they have only done the work for which God has appointed them. Such a person will always find a sphere for their zeal.[9]

The phrase "one thing" is a beautiful and biblical call to a life of priority and purpose, as we see in these passages:

- *One thing* I ask from the LORD, this only do I seek: that I may dwell in the house of the LORD all the days of my life, to gaze on the beauty of the LORD and to seek him in his temple. (Psalm 27:4)

- This *one thing* I know: God is for me! (Psalm 56:9)[10]

- *One thing* you lack . . . Go, sell everything you have and give to the poor, and you will have treasure in heaven. Then come, follow me. (Mark 10:21)

- *One thing* is needed, and Mary has chosen that good part, which will not be taken away from her. (Luke 10:42)[11]

- *One thing* I do know. I was blind but now I see! (John 9:25)

- *One thing* I do: Forgetting what is behind and straining toward what is ahead, I press on toward the goal to win the prize for which God has called me heavenward in Christ Jesus. (Philippians 3:13–14)

- Just *one thing*: Live your life in a manner worthy of the gospel of Christ. (Philippians 1:27)[12]

Living in one-day segments of obedience doesn't mean we fail to plan tomorrow's work. We need to seek God's guidance for the long haul, dream about our futures, set our objectives, establish our goals, and plan our calendars. As best we can, we need to peer into a telescope aimed at tomorrow and seek to envision what God has for us a year from now. Five years. Ten. Twenty. As my friend David Jeremiah says, "We're grateful for our memories, but our dreams should be greater than our memories. Our best work is still to come."

Yet even the most perceptive of us are like nearsighted drivers on a foggy road. We can reasonably see what's closer if we adjust our headlights accordingly, but objects farther away are blurred and the end of the road is nowhere in sight. We can see only to the end of the column of light; and only when we get there do we find illumination for the next bit of the journey.

As a physical condition, nearsightedness affects about 30 percent of the population;[13] but as it relates to the future, we're all nearsighted. We can usually make reasonable sense of today. We can anticipate our week's work. We can chart out our month. We can schedule certain events years in advance. We can envision and articulate our goals. But we can be responsible only for today. The Bible stresses the *daily* nature of faithful living, as the following verses suggest:

- Do not boast about tomorrow, for you do not know what a day may bring. (Proverbs 27:1)

- Listen, you who say, "Today or tomorrow we will go to this or that city, spend a year there, carry on business and make money." Why, you do not even know what will happen tomorrow. What is your life? You are a mist that appears for a little while and then vanishes. Instead, you ought to say, "If it is the Lord's will, we will live and do this or that." (James 4:13–15)

- Do not worry about tomorrow, for tomorrow will worry about itself. Each day has enough trouble of its own. (Matthew 6:34)

We want to make sure our vehicles are on the right roads, our maps unfolded and our guidance systems activated, our route reasonably planned, and our destination charted as clearly as possible. But we have to tackle the road one curve at a time. Our lifelong dreams are broken down into the mile markers of one-day installments, and the sweeping aspirations for our lifespans can be implemented only as we capture each day in turn for Christ. We may not be able to contend with a decade all at once, or joust with a year, or even manage a month. But we can tackle today.

Finish each day before you begin the next, and interpose a solid wall of sleep between the two. This you cannot do without temperance.

—Ralph Waldo Emerson[14]

Just for today we can be pleasantly productive. Just for today we can be faithful. Just for today we can resist temptation. Just for today we can choose to be joyful and to live for Jesus. Just for today we can be about the Father's business.

The great South African pastor Andrew Murray wrote,

A day, just one day only, but still a day, given to abide and grow up in Jesus Christ. Whether it be a day of health or sickness, joy or sorrow, rest or work, of struggle or victory, let the chief thought with which you receive it in the morning thanksgiving be this: A day that the Father gave; in it I may, I must, become more closely united to Jesus. As the Father asks, "Can you trust me just for this one day?" you cannot but give the joyful response, "I will trust and not be afraid."[15]

Much of my thinking about living one day at a time was formed by a college-age discovery of Psalm 139:16–18, which says:

> *You saw me before I was born.*
> *Every day of my life was recorded in your book.*
> *Every moment was laid out*
> *before a single day had passed.*
> *How precious are your thoughts about me, O God.*
> *They cannot be numbered!*
> *I can't even count them;*
> *they outnumber the grains of sand!*
> *And when I wake up, you are still with me!*[16]

In other words, the child of God never awakens to a day unplanned by heaven or unattended by the Lord. When the alarm goes off each morning, we roll out of bed knowing we have a divine purpose, plan, and presence. There are no blackout dates on the calendars God keeps for our lives. There are no mistakes in His almanac. "His compassions never fail. They are new every morning; great is your faithfulness" (Lamentations 3:22–23).

Those words in Lamentations were written by Jeremiah, whose outlook was surely aided by something God told him when he was a very young man, recorded in Jeremiah 1:5: "Before I shaped you in the womb, I knew all about you. Before you saw the light of day, I had holy plans for you."[17] I think those words are just as true for you as for him.

The Bible says, "As your days, so shall your strength be" (Deuteronomy 33:25).[18] Long ago, the far-famed British preacher Charles Haddon Spurgeon preached a sermon about Deuteronomy 33:25. This verse, Spurgeon observed, does not say, "As your months may demand . . . or as your years may demand." God's strength, like the manna in the wilderness, is dispensed in daily units. He said,

You are not going to have Monday's grace given you on a
Sunday, nor Tuesday's grace on a Monday. You shall have
Monday's grace given you on Monday morning as soon as
you rise and want it; you shall not have it given you on Saturday night; you shall have it day by day. . . . As thy *days*, so
shall thy strength be.[19]

Emily Huntington Miller (1833–1913) was a trailblazing Methodist
educational leader who served as dean of women students at North-
western University in Illinois. She was a prolific writer and publisher.
Her life was changed by one sentence from Bishop John H. Vincent
that she engraved on a white card in clear black type and posted on
her desk:

It meets my eyes every morning and many times during the
day . . . a resolve, not for a lifetime or a year or a month,
but just for a day; for this day; new every morning; like our
needs and God's mercies; sanctifying life by making each
day as it comes a day of holy service, without wasting regret
upon yesterday or anticipating the difficulties of tomorrow . . . Just for today.

The sentence that so impressed Emily Huntington Miller was: "I will
this day try to live a simple, sincere, and serene life."[20]

John Maxwell touches on the day-by-day nature of life in his
book *Today Matters*. "There are only a handful of important decisions people need to make in their entire lifetime," Maxwell wrote.
"If you make decisions in those key areas once and for all—and then
manage those decisions daily—you can create the kind of tomorrow
you desire. Successful people make right decisions early and manage
those decisions daily."[21]

Maxwell suggests that most people exaggerate yesterday and

overestimate tomorrow, though they have no control over either. We can't change yesterday or depend on tomorrow. Today is the only day we have. "If we want to do something with our lives, then we must focus on today," wrote Maxwell. "The secret of your success is determined by your daily agenda. . . . You will never change your life until you change something you do daily."[22] Maxwell claims he can predict who will or will not be successful simply by following them for a day or two and studying their daily agenda.

The secret to being effective, efficient, and effervescent is this biblical truth: God has a specific purpose for our lives, and when we turn aside from all else to follow God's plan, we synchronize with the sacred. Our Father has brought us into the family business, and that's what our lives must be about. We don't know the future, but we can simply pray with the hymnist: "Father, lead me day by day, ever in Thine own sweet way; / Teach me to be pure and true; show me what I ought to do."[23]

Living like this removes much stress from life, for it reminds us who is really in charge—and it isn't us. That's a load we needn't bear.

So every fresh morning, let's arise to pray in the attitude expressed in this great prayer by George Dawson (1821–76):

Almighty God, we bless and praise Thee
that we have wakened to the light of another earthly day;
and now we will think of what a day should be.
Our days are Thine, let them be spent for Thee.
Our days are few, let them be spent with care.
There are dark days behind us, forgive their sinfulness;
there may be dark days before us, strengthen us for their trials.
We pray Thee to shine on this day—the day which we may call our own.
Lord, we go to our daily work; help us to take pleasure therein.
Show us clearly what our duty is; help us to be faithful in doing it.
Let all we do be well done, fit for Thine eye to see.

Give us strength to do, patience to bear; let our courage never fail.
Help us most when faintness comes; hold us up when weariness begins.
When we cannot love our work, let us think of it as Thy task;
and by our true love to Thee, make unlovely things
shine in the light of Thy great love. Amen.[24]

Try it! Begin at once;
before you venture away from this quiet moment,
ask your King to take you wholly into His service,
and place all the hours of this day quite simply at His disposal,
and ask Him to make and keep you ready
to do just exactly what He appoints.
Never mind about tomorrow; one day at a time is enough.
Try it today, and see if it is not a day of strange,
almost curious peace, so sweet that you will be only too thankful,
when tomorrow comes, to ask Him to take it also,
till it will become a blessed habit.

—Frances Ridley Havergal[1]

3

The Most Pleasant Life Anyone Can Live

Herbert V. Prochnow, an American banking executive who became a famous toastmaster and after-dinner speaker, had a wonderful way of putting things. Regarding our core life's decisions, he said, "There is a time when we must firmly choose the course we will follow, or the relentless drift of events will make the decision."[2]

You may be the hardest-working, most productive person in the world, but if you're not living on purpose, you're caught in a relentless drift. If you're doing the wrong things, it's a life poorly spent. "It's not enough to be busy. . ." said Henry David Thoreau, "we must ask: 'What are we busy about?'"[3] The eternal God has an exciting purpose and plan for our lives—the Father's business—that can be accessed only through the lordship of Christ in day-size increments. Consider these biblical facts:

- We are not on earth haphazardly—not products of primordial sludge that randomly came to life and accidentally developed into the complexity of who we are. We're made in God's own image, and He always operates with purpose, passion, peace, and poise.

- We are on earth today because God designed an individual plan for us to be alive at this particular moment, knowing in advance the impact we can have in a world He loves. Since He is all-knowing, the past and future are equally plain to Him.

- We were each born on just the right day on His calendar, and we will finish our earthly tasks at just the right moment in His will.

- He placed us on a planet that rotates on its axis by His command once every twenty-four hours.

- He has correspondingly planned His will to unfold in one-day increments. While we do our best to ascertain what God has for us in the future and plan our calendars accordingly, we can live only in one-day increments.

- Our greatest joy is to open each day determined to invest our daily allotment of hours doing exactly what God has planned for us—being about our Father's business. If we begin each day with a prayer for His will to be done as it's done in heaven, we'll end each day bringing glory to Him.

- This pattern, pursued for a lifetime, will enable us to finish the work God has given us at the end of our earthly lives, and we'll begin our heavenly careers with the words "Well done, good and faithful servant."

- If we think of the total accumulation of all the work upon us, we'll break down. We'll be paralyzed by the weight of it all. But if we take our tasks one day at a time, we'll accomplish more than we can imagine with a minimum of strain.

- The most important day in our lives, therefore, is today. "This is the day the LORD has made; we will rejoice and be glad in it" (Psalm 118:24).[4] As J. Oswald Sanders said, "There are enough hours in each day for us to fulfill God's perfect and particular plan for our lives."[5]

The person who understands these simple bullet points lives radically differently from those who don't. The rest of the world may have a subjective, temporary sense of purpose, but as Jesus told His brothers who were not yet believers: "My time is not yet here; for you any time will do" (John 7:6). Our Lord was saying, in effect, "I have an agenda for My life and everything is on God's schedule. You don't have a divine agenda, so it doesn't matter very much what you do or when you do it."

In being committed to His Father, Jesus had a different kind of schedule; but since His brothers weren't obedient to God, what they did or when they did it wasn't as important. When our lives are set to God's course, our clocks can be wound to His schedule. When our lives aren't aligned with God's course, our hands move around uselessly.

Titus 3:14 warns, "Our people . . . should not live useless lives."[6] Without a divinely appointed purpose in life, we're devoid of a compelling reason to do anything other than eat, drink, be merry, and divert ourselves from the implications of our existential emptiness. If we don't know what we're supposed to be doing, we do lesser things, squandering ourselves on unworthy pursuits and trying to narcotize ourselves from the nagging feeling that life is essentially empty. This is the message of the Old Testament book of Ecclesiastes. Solomon, having turned from the priorities God gave him, found life utterly empty and ultimately meaningless (Ecclesiastes 1:2).

Many people waste mindless hours surfing the internet, playing computer and video games, watching TV, going to movies, engaging in idle chitchat, and frittering away their lives on nothing more than diversions. Boredom is the attitude that occurs when we fail to embrace the privilege of living a heaven-driven life. Laziness is what happens when we have no compelling cause to energize our day.

The bookstores are packed with biographies of people who achieved amazing goals or left remarkable legacies, but I think that from God's perspective many of their lives were wasted. Whenever we plunge into a crowd—at schools, churches, stadiums, workplaces, shopping malls—we're surrounded by people who spin through life like cyclones, without accomplishing what God had planned for them or the work assigned them by the Lord Jesus.

The prophet Micah warned the people of his day: "No matter how much you get, it will never be enough—/ hollow stomachs, empty hearts. / No matter how hard you work, you'll have nothing to show for it—/ bankrupt lives, wasted souls" (Micah 6:14).[7]

The world is heavily populated by wasted souls, and we instinctively know something's wrong with the direction of most of humanity. That's why there's an upsurge in philosophy courses at major universities around the world.[8] Students—befuddled by moral confusion and financial stress, lonely despite social networking, overladen with electronic gadgetry—are looking for a unifying set of principles to make sense of life.

British philosopher Paul Strathern said, "The age of seemingly ever-expanding scientific knowledge requires more than ever a philosophy to underpin that knowledge. In an overall sense this has yet to be found. Perhaps it never will."[9]

Or perhaps it has already been found, if we know where to look.

Earlier this year a thunderstorm knocked out the electricity to our house. Lighting an oil lamp, I picked up a book I'd wanted to read. It was a slim biography of the philosopher Bertrand Russell, who was born in Wales in 1872. In the flicker of the flame, I read about Russell's sad childhood. His father, mother, and sister died by the time he was five, and his grandparents took him in. But it was his elder brother, Frank, who made the biggest impact on his life by introducing him to Euclid's *Elements*, the collection of books by the famous Greek scientist about mathematics and geometry. By age eleven Russell was so enthralled with Euclid of Alexandria, he said, "I had not imagined there was anything so delicious in the world."[10]

But eventually Russell began questioning the basis of Euclid's reasoning. The ancient scholar had based his mathematical systems on certain axioms, but how do we know those axioms are true? How do we know anything is true? Russell grew confused. He went for long walks and watched the sun set over the River Thames and contemplated suicide. He later said he was searching for "something beyond what the world contains, something transfigured and infinite. . . . I have always desired to find some justification for the emotions inspired by certain things that seemed to stand outside human life and to deserve feelings of awe."[11]

Yet from his youth, Bertrand Russell dismissed the notion of a personal God—the one reality that could have given him what he most craved. Russell entered Cambridge to study mathematics but became disillusioned with what he learned. That's when he turned to philosophy. Along the way, he fell in love and married a young woman from America. But sometime later while bicycling along a country road, he decided he was no longer in love. After divorcing her, he spent his subsequent decades in a string of dissatisfactory relationships with a succession of women.

When the Bolshevik Revolution overtook the czars, Russell thought a just society was dawning at last. Traveling to Russia with high hopes, he met privately with Vladimir Lenin. But that, too, ended in disillusionment.

Bertrand Russell, who lived to be ninety-eight, was brilliant and prolific, a respected thinker. But he never found a philosophy of life that, if followed consistently, made rational sense and produced happiness. In his autobiography, he wrote these haunting words: "We stand on the shore of an ocean, crying to the night and the emptiness; sometimes a voice answers out of the darkness. But it is the voice of one drowning; and in a moment the silence returns. The world seems to me quite dreadful."[12]

As I finished Bertrand Russell's story and the lights came back on, I thought, *If only his brother had given him the Word of God in childhood instead of the* Elements *of Euclid. If only Russell had discovered there is a rational philosophy, a biblical one, which, if followed consistently, is true and leads to a positive attitude and a productive life. What if Bertrand Russell had learned to master life from the Master Himself? What if he had learned to be about the Father's business?*

I was fortunate to have been given a Bible as a child. My parents didn't have a lot of money, but my dad always made sure I had a Bible. One of my first was a little New Testament with olivewood covers, which a visiting evangelist was selling for a dollar at a church service we attended. My dad gave me a dollar, and I went up to the man and purchased one. Going home, I wrote my name in it and read it at bedtime. Later my father and I found a full-length Bible with tabs for each book and each chapter. Using those tabs, I began learning my way around the Scriptures.

I trusted Christ as my Savior in childhood and have read the Bible all my life. But as a teenager, I was pretty lazy and unmotivated. I slept late, didn't make my bed, got by on minimal amounts of studying, battled some loneliness and depression, and was easily bored and distracted. I did things only when they became urgent.

That changed one night when I was nineteen years old, at the beginning of my sophomore year at Columbia International University. After my roommate told me how Christ had totally changed his life and how I should follow his example in fully yielding my life to Christ as Lord of all, I knelt down in front of an old vinyl sofa at the end of a dormitory hallway and yielded my life to the Lord Jesus as fully as I knew how. I told the Lord I wanted Him to have His way in every part of my life, every day and every hour. I told Him I was abandoning any plans I had for my own life and adopting His will instead, trusting Him to reveal the steps to me day by day and year after year.

Crawling into bed that night, I looked out the window and saw the stars filling the sky. For the first time in my life, I was so excited about finding a sense of direction, I could hardly sleep; I couldn't wait to get up in the morning so I could go to breakfast and tell the first person I met what had happened to me. That was about forty years ago. I've not had a boring day since. It's as though an adrenaline trigger was flipped that's never switched off.

When Jesus returned to heaven, He left his servants in charge of things, "each with his assigned task" (Mark 13:34). Finding, fulfilling, and finishing the task appointed and assigned to us—whatever it is—this is our greatest and only calling in life. It's the source of our energy and enthusiasm. After all, in its original Greek, the very word translated "enthusiasm" was coined to describe the incredible attitude of the early Christians who had God in their hearts—*en* (in) *theos* (God)—en-theos-ism. There was no extant term for the new-found passions of excitement exhibited by the early disciples, so onlookers simply said, "God is in them! They are *en theos-ed* [enthused]."

We're custodians of the time God has given us. Puritan writer Richard Baxter said, "It will be an unspeakable comfort to look back on a life well spent. And to be able to say in humble sincerity, 'My time was not cast away. . . . It was spent in sincere labors for my God—in making my calling and election sure, in doing good to men's souls and bodies, it was entirely devoted to God.' "[13]

Matthew Henry, the famous commentator, said these words on his deathbed in 1714: "You have been used to take notice of the sayings of dying men. This is mine: that a life spent in the service of God and communion with Him, is the most pleasant life that anyone can live in this world."[14]

You may not have all the answers about the far-flung future; you may be frustrated with tomorrow's uncertain forecast. But just for today you can be about our Father's business. Just for today you can be pleasantly productive and enthusiastic about life.

> *Thou my daily task shalt give;*
> *Day by day to Thee I live;*
> *So shall added years fulfill,*
> *Not my own, my Father's will.*
> —Joseph Conder[15]

Study Questions for Mastering This Pattern

1. How often do you feel your life spinning out of control, and why?

_____

_____

_____

_____

2. Is a typical day in your life well planned or at the mercy of unpredictable and haphazard events?

_____

_____

_____

_____

3. Do you have a sense of what God wants you to do today, or do you feel clueless? How can you improve your efforts to be about the Father's business?

_____

_____

_____

_____

4. What one change would bring a bit more stability to your daily life?

_____

_____

_____

_____

For more help in applying these principles or for group study or staff training, download my free _Mastering Life Workbook_ at RobertJMorgan.com/MasteringLifeWorkbook.

THE SECOND PATTERN

Redeem the Time

Life is just a minute—only sixty seconds in it.

Forced upon you—can't refuse it.

Didn't seek it—didn't choose it.

But it's up to you to use it.

Give an account if you abuse it.

Just a tiny, little minute,

But eternity is in it!

—Dr. Benjamin Elijah Mays[1]

4

Life Is Just a Minute

When evangelist Billy Graham gave the invocation at the Orange Bowl in 1970, the sponsors thanked him by presenting him with the event's commemorative gift, a Bulova Accutron wristwatch with an Orange Bowl insignia on the face. Billy was grateful, but he already had a wristwatch. Returning home, he passed the Bulova on to a family member, who, a year or so later, showed it to me and said he wished he had a skin-diving watch instead. Driving into Asheville, North Carolina, I found a jewelry store and bought the best skin-diving watch I could find, and we traded. For years afterward I proudly sported Billy's Orange Bowl Bulova on my wrist.

But one day Mr. Graham's wristwatch failed. I was pursuing graduate studies at Wheaton College at the time and had a very important class at two in the afternoon. I was busy with this and that—perhaps I was studying or napping or hiring out for yard work, I don't remember—but the Accutron told me it was ten minutes till my session. I rushed across campus and ran into my classroom only to find it empty. No one else showed up. In fact, the whole building was empty. The normal classes didn't seem to be meeting. I was stupefied until I found everyone in the cafeteria. It wasn't two in the afternoon; it was suppertime. My watch had quit hours before, and I hadn't realized it. Three or four hours of my life had vanished as though they had never existed, and I hadn't noticed. I can still remember how confused I felt when a whole afternoon disappeared because of a stopped watch.

I wish I could say I never again let time get away from me, but we all know what it is to lose an afternoon or a day. Time has a way of slipping past us like a thief in the night. We all know people who miss entire seasons of life. They remind us of tires spinning in the mud. They can't seem to get any traction in life. Some manage to waste an entire lifetime. Time passes quickly even when we're about our Father's business. When we're dumb, dumbfounded, distracted, or misdirected, a lifetime can vanish like smoke in the wind.

"What is the greatest surprise you have found about life?" a university student asked me several years ago. "The brevity of it," I replied without hesitation. . . . Time moves so quickly, and no matter who we are or what we have done, the time will come when our lives will be over. As Jesus said, "As long as it is day, we must do the work of Him who sent me. Night is coming, when no one can work" (John 9:4).

—**Billy Graham**[2]

Until we appreciate the value of time and learn to manage it with skill, we can never manage ourselves. But in learning to regulate time, we learn to govern life, for life is measured in hours and minutes, just as the body is measured in pounds and ounces. Management of time is our greatest stewardship, even greater than the stewardship of our money. Time is like currency of a different realm; it's the coinage of life.

- If money is silver, time is gold.

- If material wealth can be symbolized by rubies, time can be represented by diamonds.

- If we mismanage our money, we simply try to make more of it. But there's no making any more time. When a moment is gone, it's gone forever, like sand through an hourglass. We can't rent, buy, steal, or borrow any further amounts.

- If we squander our money, we're likely to face short-term pressure, which will be immediately obvious to us; but if we squander our time, it leads to long-term loss that may not be readily apparent until it's too late.

Time is an invisible reality created by the eternal God as the vehicle in which we can fulfill His will as we travel through life. As Robert Orbin quipped, "Time flies. It's up to you to be the navigator."[3] That means, if we're going to number our days and redeem the time, we have to live on purpose. "Redeeming the time" is a biblical phrase based on the concept of redemption, as taking something back and dedicating it to a useful cause. We need a cause, a reason for being here. Our stewardship of time is the result of a well-regulated life, one that is about our Father's business. Dr. J. H. Jewett used to say, "The disciple of Christ is to be an expert merchant in the commodity of time."[4] In other words, the Lord's followers should know better than anyone else how to keep their calendars and clocks, for what they're called to do is greater than anything else.

There are three enormous time wasters that slip their palms into our pockets like thieves and rob us of our days. In my opinion, these are the biggest wasters of all *time*:

- Misdirection: Doing the wrong things.

- Laziness: Being overcome by lethargy.

- Entertainment: Being addicted to diversions of all sorts and screens of all sizes.

The final item, entertainment, may be the most pervasive time waster in our culture. Because of the world's secular philosophical choices—the implications of which it can't live with—our culture has invented millions of ways of diverting itself. Even Christians are drawn into the snare of twenty-four-hour-a-day entertainment. But it's the first of the three, misdirection, that's the most satanic. No matter how intensely we're pursuing our goals, if they don't align with the Father's will, we're wasting the lives God has given us. A basic premise of business and commerce is this: Leadership means doing the right things, whereas management means doing things right. When management does things right, we call that efficiency. When leadership does the right things, we call that effectiveness.

In our world of business, industry, and government, we need both—effective leadership and efficient management. On a personal level, it's the same. We must be doing the right things, and we need to be doing them in the best ways. This requires a keen handling of our clocks and calendars.

I wish, Sir, you would give me some instructions with regard to my time, and advise me how to proportion my Studies and my Play, in writing, and I will keep them by me and endeavor to follow them. I am, dear Sir, with a present determination of growing better.

—John Quincy Adams, ten years old, in
a letter to his father, John Adams[5]

Not long ago, I visited Greenwich, England, to research the origins of the discipline of the stewardship of time. Experts tell us that the science of time management is a relatively new phenomenon. Most prior generations had no clocks; few had sundials or hourglasses. No one "kept" time. Before the onset of the Industrial Revolution in the eighteenth century, only a few people worried about what time it was. The day began when the sun came up, and it ended when the sun went down. Days were longer in the summer, shorter in the winter, extended only by candlelight or the golden glow of a lantern. Most people worked hard because they had no other choice. It was a matter of survival. But the daily grind wasn't tied to clocks and calendars, just to the rising and retiring of the sun and the circling of the seasons.

Even after the first primitive clocks were invented, there was no standardized way to set them. Exact time measurement was possible for only one fleeting moment each day—at high noon. For a passing minute, the shadows on the ground let people know that it was the precise middle of the day, and churchwardens would run up the bell tower and adjust the clock. Since every town in Europe occupied a slightly different spot on the globe, every clock was set to a different time. Villages within a few miles of each other posted different times on the clock towers.

Meanwhile, in the New World, only about 10 percent of the population had any kind of clock in their homes when the Constitution was adopted in the United States in 1787, and few of those clocks had second hands.[6] A person's day might be crammed with tasks, but no one was looking at his or her watch or counting the seconds.

Everything changed with the invention of trains and the onset of the Industrial Revolution. The development of factories and the introduction of the rail system forced people to coordinate their schedules, resulting in clock-consciousness. When Greenwich Mean Time was adopted, it was over the protests of towns and villages all across England, which reluctantly gave up their own local ownership of standard time.

I was surprised to learn there were no time zones anywhere in the world until the railroad companies established them in the 1800s. In the United States and across Europe, time zones were devised by train companies to coordinate rail schedules. It was also the railroad system that caused people to start wearing pocket watches so they wouldn't miss their trains. Smaller versions of these pocket watches appeared on the market, designed for the wrist, but they were not popularized until about 1911, which happened to be the year my father was born. Wristwatches didn't become popular with the general public until the 1920s.[7]

For the next forty years, even people who wore wristwatches tended to speak in generalities about time. I remember my dad telling me how to answer when someone asked me for the time. He said to look down at my Mickey Mouse watch, and if the little hand was near four and the big hand was somewhere near twelve, I could round off the number and say it was four o'clock. It might have been five minutes till four or five minutes after four; it didn't matter. Most people just rounded off.

Then came the digital age, and we stopped rounding off. Our watches and clocks said 3:57. And now things are so precise that the clock in my kitchen is somehow linked by satellite to the U.S. Naval Observatory, which houses the U.S. Directorate of Time, and I know what time it is to a millimeter of a second.

It's possible to be overly obsessive about anything, and sometimes in our split-second world, we take time-consciousness to extremes. I once saw these words posted on a bulletin board: "Blessed are the flexible, for they shall not get bent out of shape." I try to remember that phrase, because I'm often bent out of shape when forced to wait in a line or for an appointment. Marilyn Monroe is reported to have quipped, "I've been on a calendar, but never on time."[8] I've never been on a calendar, but I try to live by the clock; and I'm sorry to say that I'm irritable when there aren't enough cashiers in the grocery line or when traffic is backed up on the interstate. And don't get me started about long waits in doctors' offices. I'm working on my irritability; that's not the right response. But the Bible does warn us in 1 Corinthians 7:29, "Time is short." I'm jealous of my time. Every moment comes only once, and it comes suddenly; then forever slips into the irretrievable past.

If it's important for us to be faithful stewards of our material possessions, how much wiser to be stewards of the gift of time! Every year is an opportunity, every day is a treasure, every hour is a gift, and every moment should be wisely used. In subsequent pages I'll share some ideas I've learned about redeeming the time, but it begins when we learn to appreciate the high value God places on the handfuls of moments that make up our lives. Two texts in the Bible focus all their energies on this subject, as we'll see in the next chapter. We don't know how long we'll be on earth, but we do know that every moment should be numbered and every hour redeemed for Christ and His kingdom, for Christ and His cause.

As the poet said: *Just a tiny, little minute, but eternity is in it.*

Lost wealth may be restored by industry,—
the wreck of health regained by temperance,—
forgotten knowledge restored by study,—
alienated friendship smoothed into forgetfulness,—
even forfeited reputation won by penitence and virtue.
But whoever looked upon his vanished hours,—
recalled his slighted years,—stamped them with wisdom,—
or effaced from Heaven's record the fearful blot of wasted time?

—Lydia Sigourney, nineteenth-century American poet[1]

5

The Bible's Twin Texts on Time

harles Caleb Colton was an eccentric British writer and cleric who loved global traveling, art collecting, wine tasting, and partridge shooting. He made and lost a fortune in gambling. On the side, he gave lectures about morals, and he's best remembered for his quips and quotes. He knew how to turn a great phrase, and for many years his sayings have been recycled in books like *Bartlett's Familiar Quotations*. Colton, for example, is the one who first said "Imitation is the sincerest form of flattery." On another occasion, he advised, "When you have nothing to say, say nothing."[2]

It's Colton's definition of *time* that brings him into this book. "Time," he said, "is the most indefinable, yet paradoxical of things; the past is gone, the future is not come, and the present becomes the past, even while we attempt to define it, and like the flash of the lightning, at once exists and expires." Time, according to Colton's apt definition, is "the bleak and narrow isthmus between two eternities."[3]

That reminds me of two passages in the Bible—Psalm 90 and Ephesians 5. These two portions of Scripture are about time and our custodianship of it. One occurs in the middle of the Old Testament and the other in the middle of the New. One is a prayer to offer, the other a command to obey. The first was written by Moses, the second by the apostle Paul.

Psalm 90
Number Your Days Because Time Is Short

In Psalm 90:12, Moses gave us a special prayer regarding calendar concerns, suggesting we learn to ask God's help in numbering our days so we can present Him a heart of wisdom. The superscription over the Psalm 90 passage says: "A Prayer of Moses the Man of God." Moses began in verse 1 by talking about the transcendent nature of God: "Lord, you have been our dwelling place throughout all generations. Before the mountains were born or you brought forth the whole world, from everlasting to everlasting you are God."

The phrase "from everlasting to everlasting" is mind-boggling. Eternity seems to have two infinite points at distant ends of an endless continuum. Try to imagine it. Peer into the past and into the future, knowing that neither has a commencement or terminus. There is no beginning or ending to God—only forever-ness in both directions. We could say, "From eternity past to eternity future, You are God." One man translated it, "From the vanishing point to the vanishing point."[4] Eugene Peterson, in his paraphrase of this psalm, says: "From 'once upon a time' to 'kingdom come'—you are God."[5]

From before the beginning until after the ending, God remains the same. He is infinite in both chronology and geography, that is, in both time and space. As Milton put it, God dwells in "eternity, whose end no eye can reach."[6]

Moses went on in Psalm 90 to contrast the infinitude of God with the transient life span of human beings. Compared to God's transcendence, we're as transitory as daylilies. We're like grass springing up in the morning and dying in the evening. Every human being on earth is subject to sudden death at any moment. In discussing the brevity of life, Moses wasn't talking about the eternal life we'll enjoy forever in heaven. He was saying that we've got only so much time here on earth, and not much of it.

Verse 10 says: "Our days may come to seventy years, or eighty, if our strength endures; yet the best of them are but trouble and sorrow, for they quickly pass, and we fly away."

That leads to an important prayer. We who are transitory should ask Him who is transcendent to help us be wise stewards of our swiftly passing years, days, and hours. We should pray for the skill of being shrewd managers of the commodity of time. Verse 12 suggests just such a prayer for us to sincerely offer God in light of the brevity of life: "Teach us to number our days, that we may gain a heart of wisdom."

In other words, we should pray: "Lord, keep me from wasting time. Since You are infinite and my life on earth is brief, teach me to count each day and to make each day count. May I be a good steward of every moment. May I number my days like a miser counting his coins. When You look at my usage of time, may You see a heart of wisdom."

Lost wealth may be replaced by industry, lost knowledge by study, lost health by temperance or medicine, but lost time is gone forever.

—Samuel Smiles[7]

If time be of all things the most precious, wasting time may be the greatest prodigality, since lost time is never found again. . . . Let us then be up and doing, and doing to the purpose; so by diligence shall we do more with less perplexity.

—Benjamin Franklin[8]

Ephesians 5
Redeem the Time Because the Days Are Evil

There's a parallel teaching in the New Testament epistles, where the apostle Paul writes in Ephesians 5:15–16: "Look carefully then how you walk, not as unwise but as wise, making the best use of the time, because the days are evil."[9]

Notice the commandment: "Make the best use of the time." Not just *good* use, but the *best* use. The older Bible translations use the phrase "redeeming the time."[10] Some newer versions say things like "making the most of every opportunity."[11] But the essence of the command is that we're living in urgent and evil times, and so we must live wisely.

Be careful how you live; be mindful of your steps. Don't run around like idiots as the rest of the world does. Instead, walk as the wise! Make the most of every living and breathing moment because these are evil times. So understand and be confident in God's will, and don't live thoughtlessly. Don't drink wine excessively. The drunken path is a reckless path. It leads nowhere. Instead, let God fill you with the Holy Spirit.

—Ephesians 5:15–18[12]

Because we're living in times like these, it's imperative to wisely manage our life's agendas and our daily schedules. This is the isthmus on which we live—a band of time like a narrow sandbar between the wickedness of our planet and the will of our Father. We've been given a few ticks of the clock in which to complete our tasks. Every minute counts, and we're to number our days and redeem the time that remains.

To summarize: Psalm 90 tells us God is transcendent but we are transient, so we must count our days and make our days count. Ephesians 5 tells us God is holy but the days are evil, so we must make the best use of our time. If this advice was needed thousands of years ago when the Bible was written, in an age without calendars or clocks, how much more so now! Yet we've never been more hurried or harried. Our time-saving technologies have made us busier than ever, and the sheer volume of everyday life is overwhelming our systems. I sometimes feel like Abraham Lincoln when besieged by people pestering him for government jobs at the same time the Civil War was breaking out. He said he felt like a man renting out rooms at one end of the house while the other end was on fire.[13]

But the Lord wouldn't have given us Psalm 90:12 and Ephesians 5:16 without the assurance that we can effectively offer the former as a prayer and obey the latter as a command. Now more than ever, we must ask God for wisdom in administering our schedules and redeeming the moments. It can be done through the power of Christ in us.

In Steve Jobs's famous 2005 graduation address at Stanford University, he warned the students,

> Your time is limited, so don't waste it. . . . When I was seventeen, I read a quote that said something like: "If you live each day as if it was your last, someday you'll most certainly be right." It made an impression on me, and since then, for the past 33 years, I have looked in the mirror every morning and asked myself: "If today were the last day of my life, would I want to do what I am about to do today?" And whenever the answer has been "No" for too many days in

a row, I know I need to change something. Remembering that I'll be dead soon is the most important tool I've ever encountered to help me make the big choices in life.[14]

Jobs, who professed to be a Buddhist, was expressing a sentiment that reflected Christian teaching. If we're to accomplish what God has assigned us, we cannot do it without a diligent stewardship of our clocks and calendars or a driving sense of the Father's will. What Steve Jobs perhaps never realized is this: it's our partnership with God and labor for the family business that really endures. It's our respect for His will that converts us from time wasters into meticulous stewards of our days, hours, and minutes.

Samuel Logan Brengle was a fiery Salvation Army worker of an earlier era whose books are a source of encouragement to me. In his *Soul Winner's Secret*, he urged readers to guard against wasted moments:

> James Brainerd Taylor met a traveler at a watering trough one day, and during the five minutes their horses were drinking he so preached Jesus to the stranger that he was saved and afterwards became a missionary to Africa. They met no more, and the stranger was ever wondering who the angel of mercy was that pointed him to Jesus. One day in Africa he received a box of books, and on opening a small volume of memoirs, he saw the picture of the saintly and sainted young man who was about his Father's business, and redeemed the time at that watering trough by preaching Jesus and saving a soul instead of idly gossiping about the weather.[15]

When we're about our Father's business, we're to number our days, for life is swift; we're to redeem the time for the days are evil. But in God's perfectly designed plan, there is always enough work for the days He has given us, and exactly enough days for the work He has assigned. The old couplet (attributed to C. T. Studd) rings ever true:

> *This one life will soon be past;*
> *Only what's done for Christ will last.*

A doctor was once asked by a patient who
had met with a serious accident,
"Doctor, how long shall I have to lie here?" The answer,
"Only a day at a time," taught the patient a precious lesson . . .
If time had been given to man in the form of one unbroken day,
it would have exhausted and overwhelmed him;
the change of day and night continually
recruits and re-creates his powers. . . .
Broken small and divided into fragments, he can bear them;
only the care and the work of each day have to be undertaken—
the day's portion in its day. . . .
He has only each day to be faithful for the one short day,
and long years and a long life take care of themselves,
without the sense of their length or their
work ever being a burden.

—Andrew Murray[1]

6

Living Clockwise

Syndicated columnist Harvey Mackay said, "Time is free, but it's priceless. You can't own it, but you can use it. You can't keep it, but you can spend it. Once you've lost it, you can never get it back."[2]

That's why we need to make friends with our clocks and calendars—and this is another life lesson I learned in college. Prior to arriving for undergraduate studies at Columbia International University in South Carolina, I'd never needed to worry about schedules or agendas. I drifted through life without a keen sense of purpose or planning. It's true I'd advanced from my Mickey Mouse watch to my Billy Graham one, but I didn't have a calendar to my name. My life was simple enough to keep it all in my mind—be in class every morning at 8:15 and don't forget Friday's ball game. Now, all of a sudden, I had to juggle class schedules with study time and assignment deadlines and work hours. It quickly cycloned into a sort of frantic agitation with all-nighters, near misses, and frenzied nerves.

After one particularly upsetting episode, I sat down at my desk with a piece of typing paper in the landscape position, a ruler, a pen, and a set of colored pencils. Drawing six lines down the page, I created seven columns. I drew horizontal lines for the hours and managed to capture all the waking hours of the week within the parameters of the page. Pulling out my colored pencils, I started blocking out non-negotiables, such as my class periods and required chapel times. With another color, I shaded my work schedule. After all my set obligations were in place, I looked at the white space remaining and chose some of it for study, using another color to set aside those hours. In this way, I established a regular study schedule for the first time in my life. Friday night was colored in as an evening off to do whatever I wanted. And so forth. I tacked my page to the wall by my desk and I lived by it quite faithfully. Interruptions, I learned, might disrupt the schedule, but they could be better handled within the framework of a preplanned agenda than without one.

That was forty years ago, and I'm still doing the same thing. I no longer use rulers and colored pencils. I have an electronic system on my computer and phone, and I keep a monthly at-a-glance calendar in my notebook. But the essence of the procedure is the same. It helps tremendously to keep a visual road map of time—a daily, weekly, monthly, and annual calendar, putting in the scheduled items over which we have no control, inserting the important items in a deliberate way, and letting everything else take up the remainder.

It was long after I'd graduated and entered professional life that I found this concept stated by Eugene H. Peterson. In his book *The Contemplative Pastor*, he wrote a simple sentence I've never forgotten: "The appointment calendar is the tool with which to get unbusy." His point was that busyness is an outrage. He quoted Hilary of Tours, who diagnosed busyness as *irreligiosa soicitudo pro Deo,* a blasphemous anxiety to do God's work for Him. When our schedule is packed from dawn to dusk with a thousand details, we have no time to think, ponder, pray, listen, or enjoy the abundant life. The way to escape some of the burden of busyness is through the judicious use of a personal calendar. "The trick, of course," wrote Peterson, "is to get to the calendar before anyone else does."[3]

Management experts call this the "focus block method."

Georgetown professor Cal Newport wrote, "The focus block method leverages the well-understood concept of a pre-scheduled appointment. It has you block off a substantial chunk of time, most days of the week, for applying sustained focus to your most important creative tasks. . . . The key twist is that you make this time on your calendar like any other meeting."[4]

When we block out time in our calendars for the important, then the pressing demands can fill in the gaps. Most people do the opposite, which results in what Charles Hummel called the "tyranny of the urgent."[5]

What is important in life? Time for prayer, Bible study, reading, thinking, and soul refreshment; time with our spouse; time with our children or grandchildren; time to rest; time for working on those major projects that will establish our legacy. Each morning as we review our calendar, we simply have to make sure those items are in place before the rush of the day floods our schedules. If we block off time for the truly important, we're well on the way to controlling our schedules rather than our schedules controlling us.

Marriage counselors, for example, are alarmed about the scant amount of time husbands and wives spend with each other and the time parents spend with their children. We're a distracted generation. In olden times, families spent vast chunks of time together in the farmhouse and around the barn and in the fields. Today the average family hardly has time to eat a hurried sandwich together, and that's often done in the car after we've zipped into a drive-through where someone tosses food to us through the window. I recently heard a team of counselors suggest than any marriage can be improved by committing to a 30/30 plan—spending thirty minutes together for thirty days. Another group advocates a similar 30/30 plan for running or exercise.[6] Your calendar can make those things happen if you get to it first.

Was Jesus time-conscious?

In earlier eras, the day wasn't divided into minutes, but into segments—morning, evening, hours, the watches of the night. Yet Jesus did live with a continual awareness of the Father's schedule. The Gospel of John tracks it like this:

- *"Woman, why do you involve me?" Jesus replied. "My hour has not yet come." (John 2:4)*

- *Jesus said to her, "Woman, believe me, the hour is coming. . . . The hour is coming." (John 4:21, 23)[7]*

- *They tried to seize him, but no one laid a hand on him, because his hour had not yet come. (John 7:30)*

- *Jesus said, "I am with you for only a short time." (John 7:33)*

- *No one seized him, because his hour had not yet come. (John 8:20)*

- *Jesus answered, "Are there not twelve hours of daylight?" (John 11:9)*

- *Jesus replied, "The hour has come for the Son of Man to be glorified." (John 12:23)*

- *"Now my soul is troubled, and what shall I say? 'Father, save me from this hour'? No, it was for this very reason I came to this hour." (John 12:27)*

- *Jesus knew that the hour had come. (John 13:1)*

- *Jesus looked toward heaven and prayed: "Father, the hour has come." (John 17:1)*

A thoughtfully planned schedule is the way to protect priceless moments with those people or projects most precious to us. Block in date nights, family times, camping trips, regular meals, getaway weekends, annual vacations, exercise routines, meditation rituals, and reading times with your youngsters at bedtime. Use your calendar as a shield to encircle the most important things of life.

This works for CEOs and presidents, but it's also helpful to four-year-olds. I recently taught this material to a group that included my daughter Grace, and she afterward sent me a note about the impact it had on our preschool grandson:

> I got a big dry-erase calendar to put on the fridge, and Elijah has benefited from it more than anyone. It gives him such peace of mind to see it and know when things are going to happen. And now when he asks to go to the park, or to have a day with his grandmother, instead of my giving him a vague answer, we go put it on the calendar, and then he relaxes and goes on with his day without begging or fussing.

Calendars also help us with backward goal setting. If I have a project due on, say, December 15, I look at my yearly calendar and, breaking down the project into its logical components, insert the deadlines into my schedule in advance. If it's a book deadline, I need the first chapter finished by March 1, and I need the basic draft of the whole book by November 1. Plugging these intermediate steps into my calendar helps keep the project moving.

An elaborate science has evolved around this, of course. Just consider how NASA plans a space mission with multiple operations and thousands of components all synchronized to a split second, sometimes years in advance. Corporations, organizations, businesses, and churches use complex computer models and planning grids to work backward from a launch or rollout date, making sure every component is integrated onto a comprehensive planning grid.

Few of us have projects that require labyrinthine complexity. It's just a matter of thinking ahead and giving thought to our steps. If you want to run the marathon, when do you need to start training? What do you need to do the week before the event? Two weeks before? A month before? Two months before? Insert your training schedule into your calendar. By working in reverse, you know the way forward. This is the meaning of the famous Chinese proverb, "The journey of a thousand miles begins with a single step."

Big projects can be overwhelming, but anyone can take small steps. In my book *The Red Sea Rules,* I suggest that when we're unsure what to do, we simply need to take the next logical step by faith. If we're paralyzed by procrastination and facing dilemmas that have no simple solutions, we just have to ask ourselves, "What little step can I take right now toward addressing this?"[8]

I recently read about a time management expert who claimed this idea was the greatest discovery he had ever made in wrestling control of his daily schedule. Instead of having a bunch of general items on his to-do list, he looked at every item, thought about it for a moment, and decided right then and there on the next logical step for advancing that project. He wrote down that step, plugged it into his calendar, and it became the procedure by which he kept his life progressing forward.

This isn't a book on time management techniques; there are lots of those in the library. My purpose is to emphasize a simple fact: God has given us a certain amount of work to do, and a set number of days in which to do it. If we squander the days, we'll not finish the work.

We can't go back to the days before clocks and calendars, but we can remember the words of Ralph Waldo Emerson: "Don't waste your life in doubts and fears. Spend yourself on the work before you, well assured that the right performance of this hour's duties will be the best preparation for the hours and ages that follow it."[9]

It is astonishing what a lot of odd minutes one can snatch during the day, if one really sets about it.

—Dinah Craik, nineteenth-century novelist[1]

It has been my observation that most people get ahead during the time that others waste.

—Henry Ford[2]

7

Gather the Fragments
That Remain

A small drop of ink," said Lord Byron, ". . . produces that which makes thousands, perhaps millions, think."[3] The same God who made the giant sequoias also made the tiny wildflowers that grow at their base, and both are equally beautiful. True contentment comes from enjoying the smallest pleasures of day as much as the grandest moments of the year. And true wisdom knows how to take advantage of the small drops of time that so easily fall unnoticed from our days.

While, as I said, this isn't a book on time management, I do have a practical suggestion: Do big things in small snatches of time. After Jesus had blessed and broken the lad's lunch by the lake in John 6, He filled five thousand growling stomachs and had lots of leftovers. "Gather up the fragments that remain, so that nothing is lost," He said. "Therefore they gathered them up, and filled twelve baskets with the fragments of the five barley loaves which were left over by those who had eaten" (John 6:12–13).[4]

Those aren't just random words spoken by a penny-pinching preacher or a conscientious conservationist. They represent a spiritual principle: *Gather up the fragments that remain.* Don't let anything go to waste. I don't think Jesus miscalculated in His food preparation. He wanted to demonstrate that He always provides exceedingly and abundantly, beyond all we could ask or need. He also had twelve disciples who had abandoned their livelihoods to follow Him, but whose families still needed provisions. As long as He was breaking the bread and feeding the multitudes, He made an extra basket for each of the Twelve to take home.

In applying this concept to the subject of time, that means we should gather up the small fragments of time that splinter off our main tasks. We can accomplish big things in small pieces. Dr. J. Oswald Sanders put it this way: "Stop leaks. Let us not consider our day only in terms of hours but in smaller areas of time. If we look after the minutes, the hours will look after themselves."[5]

Sometimes we pay for our purchases with twenty-, fifty-, or hundred-dollar bills. We often get smaller denominations in return, maybe a few ones or a couple of fives or a ten. Do you toss those away? Of course not. Neither should we squander five minutes here and ten minutes there. We need to make the most of the odd moments while we're waiting for an appointment, taking the train to work, stopped dead in a traffic jam, waiting for the plane to taxi to the gate, taking a coffee break, sitting in the kitchen while the microwave spins or the biscuits brown, sitting in the pew before the worship service begins.

Time, by moments, steals away,
First the hour, and then the day;
Small the daily loss appears,
Yet it soon amounts to years.

—John Newton, in his hymn "Time,
by Moments, Steals Away"

Charles Caleb Colton, a nineteenth-century English writer and wit, said, "Much may be done in those little shreds and patches of time, which every day produces and which most men throw away, but which nevertheless will make at the end of it no small deduction for the life of man."[6]

No, we don't have to be busy every moment; some of those moments are for closing our eyes, breathing deeply, relaxing our muscles, resting, praying, or meditating. Just don't waste them. Gather the fragments of time and use them. Make the most of odd moments. Take advantage of spare minutes. Don't waste your waits. Henry David Thoreau warned that we cannot kill time without injuring eternity. His exact words were, "As if you could kill time without injuring eternity."[7]

Dr. Charles Eliot, the longest-serving president in the history of Harvard University, frequently asserted that anyone could obtain the elements of a good liberal education by spending fifteen minutes a day reading from a collection of enduring books. A New York publisher saw an opportunity in that statement and suggested that Dr. Eliot compile a list of such books, which led to the famous *Harvard Classics*—a fifty-one-volume anthology of great literature, designed to be read in fifteen minutes a day.

To quote Oswald Sanders again: "It is amazing how much reading can be squeezed into fragments of time redeemed from the trash pile. It is vain to wait until we get time to read seriously—we will never get it. We must make time to read by seizing the minutes we have. . . . Detect unsuspected leakages of time, and with purpose of heart, plug the leak."[8]

It's not just reading; it's writing. When I first began a writing career, I read several books on the subject of composing books for publication. The best advice came from those who said writers only fail when they fail to write. One professor suggested devoting fifteen minutes a day to a novel or article or book. He told his students to set an egg timer for fifteen minutes and to devote that period each day to writing. Some popular fiction writers claim their best novels were written in fifteen-minute blocks of time.

There's a famous set of commentaries that has enriched Bible students and ministers for more than a hundred years. The volumes were written by Albert Barnes, and they bear his name—*Barnes' Notes*. He wrote them by devoting time to the task every morning before breakfast.

Pediatrician William Carlos Williams wrote his far-famed poetry at his desk during his lunch hours.

When he was president, Ronald Reagan would use spare moments to clean out his desk drawers. Somehow this simple act of decluttering seemed to give him a lot of pleasure.[9]

And this practice does not apply just to reading and writing; it works for anything. One of my favorite cookbooks is titled *Artisan Bread in Five Minutes a Day*. One of my favorite leadership books is *The One-Minute Manager*. I've been thinking about buying the book on developing killer abs in four minutes a day, but I'm a bit skeptical of that one.

Lifelong scripture memory can occur in a few minutes per day. Publisher Brad Waggoner grew up on a ranch where all the farmhands and cowboys carried cans of tobacco in their back pockets. Later in the military, he met a group of Christians—Navigators—who also had something outlined in their hip pockets, but it wasn't tobacco. These men carried around packets containing memory verses, which they reviewed during spare moments. Enticed to try it for himself, Brad started by memorizing three verses. "I couldn't believe what an effect they had on me, on both my thinking and my talking," he said. Brad was so motivated by the experience that he's become a lifelong advocate of scripture memory, and the verses he's learned over the years are reflected every day in the conversations he has with friends and coworkers.[10]

At a recent seminar, I chatted between sessions with a man from Vermont. I discovered he worked on a ferryboat that crosses Lake

Champlain. He said the crossing takes about one hour, and he has to work furiously for fifteen minutes of that hour. The other forty-five are free. "That's when I do my Bible study," he said.

You can also clean and declutter in small chunks. I don't often watch television, but some evenings Katrina and I have a leisurely supper and then watch a program. I've found that the commercials are longer than some of the shows they're sponsoring, and I can jump up during each break and clean the kitchen. During ads, I can clear the table, put away the leftovers, load the dishwasher, wipe off the stove and countertops, unload the dishwasher, and put away the china and silverware—without missing a minute of our program.

I might struggle some with workaholism, but I'm not advocating constant busyness. Sometimes we need to stay in the recliner, mute the commercials, and rest our nerves. I simply want us to think of the value of each passing moment. It only takes a moment to hug a loved one, to write a thank-you note, to scan an article, to read a paragraph, to whisper a prayer, to wash a dish, to file a paper, to smile at a stranger, to cuddle a baby, to rest your eyes, to conceive an idea, to learn the next word of a verse, to straighten a pillow, to text a message of encouragement.

One day after I'd spoken on this subject, my friend Charles Hingst, who is in his nineties, approached me. He told me of some words he'd read years ago that had instantly affixed themselves to his memory and had helped guide his life:

LOST
Somewhere between sunrise and sunset,
Two golden hours, each set with sixty diamond minutes.
No reward is offered, for they are lost forever.

In subsequent chapters, I'll share with you the simple morning-by-morning technique I use to maintain wise stewardship over the time God has given me. But here's the point for now: Don't let the hours flitter away and don't toss away the moments. When you've invested the hours and tackled the big tasks, gather the fragments that remain, so that nothing is lost.

You can do a lot with life's spare change.

Study Questions for Mastering This Pattern

1. What do you think it means to number your days and redeem the time?

_____

_____

_____

_____

2. Are some significant time-wasters hidden among your habits? What are they?

_____

_____

_____

_____

3. How can you more effectively employ a calendar system in managing your schedule?

_____

_____

_____

_____

4. Determine one simple way to better utilize small fragments of time and put them to use.

_____

_____

_____

For more help in applying these principles or for group study or staff training, download my free _Mastering Life Workbook_ at RobertJMorgan.com/MasteringLifeWorkbook.

THE THIRD PATTERN

Clear the Decks

> *With many, much time is lost for want of system.*
> *Things are done haphazard[ly],*
> *duties are performed at random,*
> *and after one thing is done,*
> *time is wasted in deciding what to do next.*
> *It is well, then, to have a program for every day.*
>
> —Samuel Logan Brengle in his 1903 book, *The Soul-Winner's Secret*[1]

8

God Is Not Disorganized—
Why Are You?

While on a speaking engagement in Texas recently, I met Jim
Furgerson of San Antonio. As an aviator in the U.S. Marine
Corps, Jim flew more than eight hundred missions in Vietnam and
was given the nickname Able, because he always seemed able to return unharmed with his crew. He was especially adept at landing his
plane on aircraft carriers, which is the most difficult kind of landing in the world. Pilots landing on carriers travel at a precise speed,
sometimes at night or in inclement weather, and must touch down
on a small strip that may be bobbing or weaving, depending on sea
conditions.

"I made 137 landings on carriers, including ten at night," Jim
told me, "and the 137th was just as scary as the first. In making a
landing there are three instruments that are critical, and a pilot has
to check each of those instruments one time every second as he or
she approaches the carrier. The phrase 'Clear the decks' doesn't just
mean to get other planes or heavy equipment and service personnel
out of the way. It means the area must be totally clean. These landings are so intense, so sudden, and so precise that even a plastic coffee cup or piece of glass can be disastrous. The deck has to be
absolutely free from the slightest debris to insure a safe landing."[2]

Whether it's the deck of an aircraft carrier, the desk in your office, the bench in your workshop, your laundry room, your studio,
your classroom, or your makeup table, you can't get much done if

you don't have a reasonably clear workspace. You can't find your stuff or spread out your current task. A cluttered workspace creates a confused mind. According to the National Association of Professional Organizers, Americans waste between six and twelve weeks a year searching for things in their homes and workplaces.[3]

When we ponder the attributes and nature of Almighty God, we often praise Him for His love, His grace, His majesty, His wisdom, and His power. We echo the songs of the angels who proclaim, "Holy, Holy, Holy!" But no one has ever composed a hymn that says, "Organized, Organized, Organized!" Yet organization is one of God's essential traits. The Bible says, "God is not one who likes things to be disorderly and upset. He likes harmony. . . . Be sure that everything is done properly in a good and orderly way" (1 Corinthians 14:33, 40).[4]

God is not disorganized, and when Jesus ministered on earth, His work was methodical and orderly. In the last chapter, I referred to the Lord's feeding the five thousand with loaves and fish. This is the only miracle reported by all four Gospels, so by comparing the accounts we can observe some interesting details. Mark tells us Jesus had everyone sit down in organized groups of fifties and hundreds so the food could be distributed in a swift and suitable way. According to John's Gospel, after the meal Jesus had the place cleaned up with all the leftovers going into baskets so that nothing would be wasted and no litter would remain.[5] Everything was done with planning and precision.

We're not given a lot of information in the Bible about the Lord's personal habits, His grooming, or His appearance. But in reading the Gospels we glimpse that He was meticulous in His methods and well-kept in his manner. In John 20, Peter and John ran to His tomb on Easter Sunday and found it empty—but not quite. The body of Jesus was missing, but His grave clothes were still there, as though His body had just risen out of them. The Bible says,

"Simon Peter . . . entered the tomb, observed the linen cloths lying there, and the kerchief used to cover his head . . . neatly folded by itself. Then the other disciple, the one who had gotten there first [John], went into the tomb, took one look at the evidence, and believed."[6]

When Jesus rose from the dead, He evidently took time to arrange the scarf that had been around His head. His companion John took one look at it and recognized the Lord's handiwork. Even amid the chaotic excitement of His resurrection, Jesus moved with order and organization, not confusion and chaos, leaving behind a small clue. He could not have done otherwise, for "God is not a God of confusion. . . . [Therefore] all things must be done properly and in an orderly manner."[7]

When the apostle Paul wrote those words to the Corinthians, he was talking about church services. The public gatherings in Corinth had evidently deteriorated into spiritual free-for-alls, without method or any modus operandi. People were shouting, interrupting, coming, going, and acting like a disorderly horde. Such exhibitions, Paul warned, didn't reflect the personality of God. Worship services should be exciting, fresh, sometimes spontaneous, and always God-centered. But we can do without chaos and confusion.

It seems to me this principle applies to everything we do. Think of the areas of your own life—your finances, bank statements, work areas, closet, kitchen, car, desk—and say these words: "God is not a God of confusion, therefore all things must be done properly and in an orderly manner." That's a hallmark of being pleasantly productive.

Everything we know about God, both in nature and in Scripture, supports the thesis that God is the Creator of organizational systems, and everything He does displays remarkably organized patterns. The concept of *organization* is built into the very fabric of the universe—from the design of a spider's web to the arrangement of the stellar systems. Whether you study a human cell in a microscope or the Milky Way through a telescope, you find concordance and congruity. You see coordination. All creation reflects the genius of a mind of order and infinite intelligence.

When we turn to the Bible, we see the same. The story of Moses leading the children of Israel out of Egyptian slavery and into the Promised Land occupies the books of Exodus, Leviticus, Numbers, Deuteronomy, and Joshua. At every point and in every chapter, we see God taking a chaotic mass of ex-slaves—perhaps millions of them—and organizing them into a well-functioning nation that would serve as His channel of redemption for the world.

While the Israelites were still at Sinai in Exodus 18, a national political structure and judicial system were put into place. As the chapters progress, laws were given to govern the civil operations of the nation. The last part of Exodus and all of Leviticus describe setting up the worship patterns of the people.

In Numbers, an army was conscripted. The population was divided into units, a census was taken, and the placement of the tribes around the tabernacle was prescribed in exacting detail. If you had flown over this mass of humanity in a helicopter, you would have seen neat rows of tents, arranged by tribes and encircling the tabernacle in a symmetrical pattern. Also in Numbers, the priests and their fellow officials were put into place.

In the book of Deuteronomy, the up-and-coming generation was given its heritage in written form. In Joshua, the land was divided among the various tribes, boundaries were drawn, and the Promised Land was occupied in a purposeful and progressive manner.

Talk about nation building! When the Israelites passed through the Red Sea, they had no laws or rules, no governing structures, no religious habits or cultural mores. By the time they passed through the Jordan River to possess the land, they were a well-organized people with national machinery and centralized operations. Step by step and system by system, the Lord brought order and structure to the Israelites, transforming them from a frenzied multitude to a functioning nation.

Reading elsewhere in the Bible, we notice how the legions of heavenly angels are organized, as is the church in the New Testament. Paul sent Titus to the undisciplined church of Crete to "put in order what was left unfinished and appoint elders in every town, as I directed you" (Titus 1:5).

In both church and home, the Bible provides an organizational structure that gives purpose, order, and arrangement. The Bible itself is the best-organized book ever written. The more I study it, the more I'm awestruck by its symmetry, arrangement, progression of thought, unity of theme, and brilliance of composition.

The reason the universe, the Bible, and all the works of God are so well ordered is because of the nature of the Trinity. God Himself is organized—Father, Son, and Holy Spirit—in mysterious ways we can never fully fathom. He is eternally productive, proficient, profitable, and powerful. Because He is well ordered, His works show method and appropriate tidiness.

The characters of the Bible understood the value of organization:

- Moses picked competent men from all Israel and set them as leaders over the people who were *organized* by the thousand, by the hundred, by fifty, and by ten. (Exodus 18:25)[8]

- Saul *organized* the troops. (1 Samuel 15:4)[9]

- David *organized* his forces. (2 Samuel 18:1)[10]

- When Joab saw he was under attack in front and behind he took the select troops of Israel and *organized* them. (2 Samuel 10:9)[11]

- King David also ordered the Levite leaders to *organize* the singing into an orchestra. (1 Chronicles 15:16)[12]

- [Solomon] *organized* the daily work for the priests ... in singing hymns and in doing their work. He also *organized* the Temple guards. (2 Chronicles 8:14)[13]

- *Organize* yourselves. (2 Chronicles 35:4)[14]

- I *organized* the orders of service for the priests and Levites so that each man knew his job. (Nehemiah 13:30)[15]

- Why are we sitting here, doing nothing? Let's get *organized*. (Jeremiah 18:14)[16]

- When it comes to the church, [Christ] *organizes* and holds it together, like a head does a body. (Colossians 1:18)[17]

Since you and I are the chief works of this organized God, there should be discipline and order in our lives. And that's why I don't think God wants us to live in a mess or pursue our work amid chaos or runaway clutter. Companies, corporations, and governments on every level need administrators who oversee effective sets of systems to keep their organizations moving forward according to principles flowing from the very nature of God.

Having an organized life doesn't mean we become robotic. The purpose of organization is to provide a structure for creativity, risk, experimentation, vibrancy, and improvisation. It's not an end in itself. It simply enhances everything else around us. Simply put, we're more pleasantly productive when we can find our stuff and work in an unsullied environment.

Anyone who knows God, even slightly, would ex-
pect God to make an orderly world
because God Himself is the essence of order.
God was never the author of disorder—
whether it be in society, in the home,
or in the mind or body.

—A. W. Tozer[18]

Is there an area of your life that needs an organizational make-over? We can't be pleasantly productive or finish the work God has given us without some level of organization and order. Recently I tried to stress this to a young man who is passionate about serving the Lord but decided to leave his first assignment in discouragement. He moved back home and got a job in a warehouse. When I met him I asked, "Did you make your bed today?"

It wasn't a question he expected, but he answered honestly. "No," he said. "My room's a mess."

"Well," I said, "that's where we need to start in recovering your morale and ministry." He called me the next week, and as we ended our conversation he said, "By the way, I've been making my bed every morning."

I wasn't so concerned about his bed, but about the general order of his life.

Some time later I was gratified to read a similar suggestion by Special Operations Commander, Admiral William McRaven. Speaking to graduates of the University of Texas, Austin, he described the lessons he had learned from his training as a Navy SEAL:

Every morning we were required to make our bed to perfection. It seemed a little ridiculous at the time, particularly in light of the fact that we were aspiring to be real warriors, tough battle-hardened SEALs, but the wisdom of this simple act has been proven to me many times over.

If you make your bed every morning you will have accomplished the first task of the day. It will give you a small sense of pride and it will encourage you to do another task and another and another. By the end of the day, that one task completed will have turned into many tasks completed. Making your bed will also reinforce the fact that little things in life matter. If you can't do the little things right, you will never do the big things right. And if by chance you have a miserable day, you will come home to a bed that is made—that you made—and a made bed gives you encouragement that *tomorrow* will be better.

If you want to change the world, start off by making your bed.[19]

My primary point isn't to tell you to be organized or how to achieve it. Lots of books and articles do that. Every year, surveys of New Year's resolutions put "Get organized" high on the list, right behind "Lose weight" and "Exercise more." The contribution I'd like to make to the discussion is to emphasize *why* we crave an organized life. It's because our Creator is organized in His very nature, and He has built efficient organizational structures and systems into all He has done. When we're disorganized and confused, we're operating counter to how God made us. Living in a bright and well-kept environment lifts our spirits and self-esteem. We feel better about ourselves when we keep an orderly work surface and live simply and neatly.

My friend George Westover was stationed on board the USS *Tennessee,* anchored in Pearl Harbor in December of 1941. The *Ten-*

nessee was moored alongside the *West Virginia* and directly in front of the *Arizona*. Westover was a marine private, and his salary was twenty-one dollars a month (minus eighty cents for health insurance). He loved being in Hawaii. It was peaceful, quiet, beautiful, and relaxing. He and his buddies could get a taxi into town for a dollar, which, by cramming five of them into the vehicle, would amount to twenty cents each, plus another nickel for the tip.

On Friday, December 5, 1941, Westover arrived back on the *Tennessee* a half hour late, at 8:30 pm. So he was assigned punishment duty and had to paint his battle station on Saturday, December 6. He was done with the job that evening, but he failed to seal and stow his can of gray paint. He just left it sitting there with the lid off. The next morning, December 7, 1941, he woke up anticipating the day since it was a "Ropeyarn Sunday," when sailors and marines could relax aboard ship, reading and writing letters and getting haircuts and mending their socks, or whatever. Breakfast that morning was cold cuts, baked beans, and salad. After breakfast, George decided to sunbathe, so he put on his swimming trunks, got his blanket and book, and went to a sunny spot on deck to read.

He heard the sounds of explosions over on Ford Island and he and some others stood at the railing and looked in that direction. "This is a heck of a time to have a drill and not tell us anything about it," they said among themselves. Suddenly the loudspeakers sounded on the *Tennessee*: "All hands, man your battle stations. This is no drill. This is war!" George rushed back to his quarters, threw on shirt, pants, and shoes, and returned to his place high on the ship. When he ran in, he knocked over the unattended can of paint, which made a mess and leaked onto the decks below. He had to man his station while sliding around in wet paint.

Seventy-three years later, when talking about the attack on Pearl Harbor, he still remembers how frustrating it was to fight the enemy while slipping in a pool of gray paint that seeped into shoes, stuck to his skin, got on his weapons, and dripped onto the sailors below. If he had it to do over again, he told me, he would have sealed and stowed his paint at the end of the job the day before.

Let's do a little better about stowing our stuff. Just a small improvement can make a difference. If God used clean and creative organizational principles when creating the universe, when building the nation of Israel, when feeding the multitudes in Galilee, in exiting the tomb on Easter Sunday, in directing the church work in Corinth and Crete—if He is, in fact, by nature an organized God—is there some area of your life you need to bring under His discipline and direction?

God is not disorganized. Why are you? Is there a can of paint you can seal and stow? What little area of life can you tackle today? Where is the first obvious place for you to start in bringing order and function to your day?

*In Thine own good time, so order the things
in our life that we may end in the calm, quiet peace
of those whose hearts are stayed upon God.*

—George Dawson (1821–76)[1]

9

Put Your Tray Tables in Their Upright Positions

I can get a lot of work done on an airplane. Someone else is driving the vehicle, after all, and I have no responsibility except to buckle my seat belt and locate the nearest exit in case of an emergency. I prefer window seats. They give me a good view, a wall to lean against, and privacy to one side. If my introversion is acting up, I put in my earphones, signaling unsociability. At my feet is a slender backpack with reading material, pens, schedules, writing pad, and my Bible. Every few minutes, a smiling person comes by to refill my coffee or cart away my trash. Best of all, I can lower my tray table and find a small and uncluttered work surface. It's just big enough for my book or Bible, a notepad or electronic tablet, and my coffee. With few interruptions I'm able to plug away at some little project. At the end of the flight, I'm instructed to clear my workspace and return my tray table to its full and upright position.

We begin every flight with a clear workspace, and we end it that way by putting things up. If that works in the air, why wouldn't it work on the ground? It does. Without realizing it, some long-forgotten airline executive or federal bureaucrat summed up a great rule for life in the words: "Please put your tray tables in their full and upright positions."

Like so many of the other suggestions in this book, I began learning the wisdom of this in college. My branch of the Morgan family tree has an unfortunate predisposition toward messiness. My uncle Walter's house was the worst. I visited him nearly every day and always had to wade through a sea of junk to cross the living room. He was a "junkie" in the truest sense of the word. My father would have been just as bad except that my mom was a diligent homemaker, who also hired out some of the work to a lady who tidied my bedroom every day. But when I moved into the dormitory, my domestic help didn't go with me. My side of the room deteriorated quickly. My roommate, on the other hand, was a military brat whose dad had insisted on army-grade spit-shine tidiness.

One day Bill looked at my side of the room and said in a tone that got my attention, "You can't possibly get any work done at that desk. You've got to clear everything off, reshelve your books, refile your folders, get it organized. And when you finish each task put everything up where it belongs so your desk will be clear for your next project."

He was so insistent I complied, and I learned a crucial lesson: Clear your desk after every task. Put your seatback tray table in its full and upright position. This is the simple secret to a well-ordered life, and that's why it's vital to teach our children to make their beds, pick up their toys, and keep their rooms clean. When we instill those simple organizational habits into their lives at a young age, we're giving them the skills they'll need to handle the heavier matters of life later on. We're helping them to establish a well-ordered life.

I'm not talking about obsessive neatness. I read an article the other day about organizing a refrigerator. The accompanying picture showed a fridge with the door open and everything lined up in special containers with labels and dates and regular sizes, all stacked and lined up as if a perfectionist had devoted the whole day to the chore. It was ridiculous. When we overorganize our spaces, we don't have time to maintain the systems we create and the whole apparatus crashes. Too much organization becomes counterproductive because we can't keep it up. Everything should be done with minimal complexity and maximum simplicity.

But we do have to create an appropriate level of orderliness and organization, and then we must consistently put things away. At the end of a project—whether it's taking a bath or launching a rocket into space—we have to clean up and clear out. Pick up your toys. Hang up your clothes. Make your bed. Clear your desk. Empty the dishwasher. Sort your mail. File your receipts. Return your books to their place. Empty your in-box. Hang your keys on the hook. Put the bathroom towel back on the rack. Put the dishes back on their shelves and the tools back in the box. Keep the flashlight in the bedside drawer.

Live by the maxim *A place for everything, and everything in its place.* A little maintenance each day goes a long way, and our weekly "day off" (Saturday for me) is a good time to devote a little extra effort to decluttering and reorganizing.

My friend Reese Kauffman, president of Child Evangelism Fellowship, was a successful Indianapolis manufacturer whose factories produced products for America's leading companies. He regularly visited an IBM building in Lexington, Kentucky, where he always noticed that every desk in the entire place was clear and neat. Asking about it, he was told the corporate executive had a rule that each desk had to stay absolutely clear except for the specific project the person was currently working on. That way the person's attention would be focused purely on the work at hand, and each task would be processed or finished before another was begun. It proved a successful strategy for the company.

This "clean space" philosophy includes throwing things away and reducing clutter. According to John 15, God prunes the grapevines in His vineyard and tosses away every branch that doesn't bear fruit. Every gardener knows the shrubs must be periodically pruned, otherwise they grow out of control and become less productive. Decluttering is that process by which the logistics of our lives remain manageable. Sometimes it's hard to throw things away, but at some point we're going to leave it all anyway; we might as well begin simplifying now.

I've learned a lot about this from travel expert Rick Steves. He's a great advocate for traveling light, and based on his advice I've completely changed the way I travel. I no longer take a suitcase. When the zipper broke on my old luggage, I tossed it in the trash and bought a backpack. I've learned that on most trips, I can take everything I need in a backpack or carry-on.

Traveling light isn't a new concept. It was the philosophy advocated by Henry David Thoreau in his classic book *Walden*, published in 1854. Thoreau said we should live so compactly that if an enemy overtook our town we could, like the old philosopher, "walk out the gate empty-handed and without anxiety."[2] Thoreau said, "In short, I am convinced, both by faith and experience, that to maintain oneself on this earth is not a hardship but a pastime if we will live simply and wisely." Thoreau's famous advice was "Simplify, simplify!"[3]

I once had a staff member who organized his working life twice each year. I could tell what month it was by watching his office. It became more and more disastrous till it reached a certain critical mass. By then, it looked as if someone had emptied several attics' worth of boxes, clothes, books, and debris and dumped them into his office. At that point my friend would totally empty the room, hauling every item, every book, every piece of clothing and furniture and equipment out into the hallway. We'd bring in a Dumpster, and he'd start going through things, throwing away two-thirds of it and carting the remaining third back into his office, where he situated it in a pristine way. When he finished, his office looked like a picture from a magazine. But he didn't have a system of regular maintenance, so from the moment he reopened his office, it started deteriorating until, six months later, he would have to go through the exhausting exercise again.

At least he had the right idea. The first thing you have to do is get organized. One efficiency expert said when an executive hires him to regain control of his or her life, he begins much the way my friend did. He has the executive schedule a two- or three-day block of uninterrupted time to tackle all the piles of paper and the to-do lists and clear them out of the way. For some people, this may take most of a week.

During this process, it's important to set up receptacles so everything has its logical place. We need to design places for everything so we'll know where it is. This might require a filing cabinet for your papers, a tray for your silverware, a sheet of pegboard for your shop, a box for your photographs, a kit for your sewing, or a newly designed closet system for your clothes. Companies sell organizational systems for every conceivable area of life—crates, boxes, files, folders, notebooks, shelves, cubbyholes, and cupboards—because we can't function without containers, filing cabinets, and closet systems. We need to be able to put things in a place where we can easily retrieve them when we need them. Otherwise we spend half our lives losing things and the other half looking for them.

Be regular and orderly in your life . . . so that
you may be violent and original in your work.
—Gustave Flaubert[4]

You may not be able to tackle every area of your life at once. In the Pentateuch, the Lord organized one area at a time with the Israelites.

But find an area right now—maybe your desk, your finances, your bedroom, your closet, your car, your to-do lists, the organization chart at work, the chore chart for your kids, the in-box in your office—and do what God did at the Flood or Jesus with the temple—do some cleansing. Take an hour or a day or a week, however long it takes, and get organized. And then put a sign over the whole thing saying: *God is not a God of confusion. Everything must be done properly and in an orderly manner.*

Napoleon Bonaparte reportedly said, "The battlefield is a scene of constant chaos. The winner will be the one who controls the chaos."[5] You don't have to be a perfectionist about it; it's better if you're not. Proverbs 14:4 allows for some messiness in life, saying, "Without oxen a stable stays clean, but you need a strong ox for a large harvest."[6] In other words, being clean and neat isn't the goal. We need productivity, and that requires oxen, and oxen are messy. But if we don't occasionally muck out the stable, our work suffers and our environment grows toxic. Being pleasantly productive requires having the self-discipline to regularly—not perfectly, but regularly—keep our work surfaces clean and our tray tables in their full and upright position. GO stands for Get Organized.

> "I never could have done what I have done
> without the habits of punctuality, order, and diligence, without the
> determination to concentrate myself on one subject at a time."
>
> — Charles Dickens, in *David Copperfield* [1]

> "A solid routine fosters a well-worn groove for one's mental
> energies and helps stave off the tyranny of moods."
>
> —Mason Currey, in *Daily Rituals* [2]

10

Don't Be Listless

In the early 1930s, the Boeing Company determined to build an airborne version of a U.S. Navy battleship. Employing the world's best aerodynamic engineers, the company designed and built Model 299, the Flying Fortress, the most advanced bombardment plane ever conceived, with four engines, a central bomb bay, gunnery stations, and the ability to fly over long distances at very fast speeds.

On October 30, 1935, a large group of civilian and military dignitaries gathered to watch the test flight at Ohio's Wright Field. The Flying Fortress taxied down the runway with no problem, took off beautifully, and entered a steep climb. Then, stalling, it suddenly tipped wing over wing, nosedived, and crashed in a fiery explosion, killing the two pilots. A subsequent investigation revealed that the aircraft had performed perfectly, but the pilots had forgotten to release the elevator lock prior to takeoff. The plane, it seemed, was too complex to fly: there were too many things to remember.

Trying to keep Boeing in business, a group of pilots began meeting to solve the problem. From their discussions came one of the greatest inventions of the twentieth century—the pilot's checklist. Since it was impossible to remember every detail of flying these complex planes, a checklist was needed to make sure every detail was covered, and covered in sequence. The creation of the pilot's checklist caused a revolution in airline technology and made it possible for further advancements to continue. At first, some pilots resented the checklist. But the tool has become an invaluable part of aviation history, and today even the smallest airplanes have checklists for every phase of takeoff, flight, and landing.

As our lives become busier, we have to take a page from the cockpit. We can't remember all the things we need to do. We can't intuitively do them in the proper sequence or priority. We need checklists—some way of recording our obligations, thoughts, ideas, tasks, and everything else that weighs on our minds.

In reading the Bible I get the idea the Lord loves checklists too. Take the Ten Commandments, for example. The Lord summarized all our moral obligations in life in one ten-item list that even children can memorize (Exodus 20:1–17). Jesus began His ministry with a list, which we call the Beatitudes—the nine attitudes that characterize citizens of His kingdom (Matthew 5:1–12). The apostle Paul gave us a ninefold list of attitudes to develop—the fruit of the Spirit: love, joy, peace, patience, kindness, goodness, faithfulness, gentleness, and self-control, listed in Galatians 5:22–23. On the reverse side of the ledger are the Seven Deadly Sins, listed in Proverbs 6:16–19.

The Bible is full of lists, and they help us to think through our opportunities and obligations. The book of Proverbs says, "The wisdom of the prudent is to give thought to their ways. . . . The prudent give thought to their steps" (Proverbs 14:8, 15). Proverbs 21:29 adds, "Good people think carefully about what they do."[3]

It helps when we inventory our ways, jot down our thoughts, itemize our tasks, and evaluate our priorities. Whether we're an FBI agent studying the Ten Most Wanted List, a TSA officer looking at the No Fly List, a student going over the assigned reading list, an aging adventurer trying to fulfill his bucket list, a homemaker with a grocery list, or a theologian studying Luther's 95 Theses, we can track things better with those little numbers and bullet points running down the page.

This is the central idea I took away from David Allen's popular book *Getting Things Done: The Art of Stress-Free Productivity*. After discussing the accelerating pace of our ever-changing lives, he wrote, "We haven't been well equipped to deal with this huge number of internal and external commitments."[4] He claims that our minds are overwhelmed with the sheer amount of data we face, and the only way to manage it is by keeping some sort of evolving list. "I suggest that you write down the project or situation that is most on your mind at this moment," he said, adding that we should "write down the very next physical action required to move the situation forward."[5] We have to have a receptacle or tool for "capturing all the things that need to get done—now, later, someday, big, little, or in-between—into a logical and trusted system outside of your head and off your mind."[6]

That involves some self-disciplined note-taking. Douglas C. Merrill, former chief information officer of Google, makes a similar point. "Our short-term memories can hang on to only between five and nine things, max, at one time. If you try to store ten things in short-term memory, it will drop something." That's why, Merrill insists, it's important "to get stuff out of your head as quickly as possible."[7]

I'm not going to suggest how to do this. I have my own crude methods, which involve multiple lists on my computer. I have lists for everything from groceries to birthdays; from books I want to read to books I want to write. I have to-do lists and prayer lists. Every morning I create a small but very special list to slip into my pocket as I leave my room in the morning (more about that later).

But the essence of what I'm saying is simple. Lists are biblical. Lists are basic. We have to keep them simple, but with a bit of thought we can use them more effectively than we think. For everyday living, the back of an envelope might do. For major projects, we need detailed plans. But without managing our lists, we'll be like the farmer who woke up on a bright morning and looked out the window at the back fields, which needed plowing. He headed toward the barn to start his tractor, but on his way out he noticed the screen door squeaked; so he went to find his oil can. En route to the tool shed, he noticed a loose screw on the garden gate. In the shed, he grabbed his oil can and screwdriver, but he saw weeds growing in the pathway, so he also grabbed his hoe. He finally got the door oiled, the gate tightened, and the weeds hoed; but, having his hoe in hand, he decided to putter in the flower bed. He needed his shovel to dislodge a rock; and while fetching it from the barn he noticed that the stall needed mucking out. This reminded him to replenish the oats for the horse; so he jumped into his truck and headed to the local Feed-and-Seed. He stopped for coffee next door in the diner. By the time the old fellow made it to the fields, it was too dark to plow.

Before dismissing the farmer as mindless, ask yourself, *How much of my day was spent reacting to random events as they occurred rather than pressing ahead with a definite agenda? Am I living an impromptu life, or am I consciously going about my Father's business?* We need some kind of agenda for our lives, and we need to find a way of sticking to it most of the time. Otherwise the urgent becomes intermingled with the important, and soon we'll be unable to distinguish the two.

How much better an example is the Old Testament hero Nehemiah, who shouldered the responsibility of rebuilding the walls of Jerusalem during a period of conflict and danger. The first thing he did, after praying earnestly and arriving in Jerusalem, was to inspect the walls and to think through the project.

Nehemiah conducted a nocturnal inspection of the broken walls and formulated a plan in his own mind. After thoroughly thinking it through, he was ready to lead others in the project. He laid out the project in sequential steps, explained them plainly, listed the tasks, and mobilized his people for the job. Nehemiah listed the difficulties, listed the steps to overcoming them, listed the people who were mobilized, listed his enemies, listed his coworkers, and listed each segment of the wall and who was building it. In the process his book became one of the best case studies of leadership in the history of literature.

In a popular Tom Clancy novel, one of the characters continually jotted notes in a small notebook. "You have to get used to me," she said apologetically. "Whenever I have an idea, I write it down right away." It isn't safe, she explained, to entrust important matters to memory alone, adding, "If you don't write it down, then it never happened."[8]

We can't possibly keep everything in our minds; when we try to do so, it creates endless interior tension. We suffer the nagging feeling we're forgetting things, which we probably are. When we go to bed, we suddenly remember something needing to be done. When we get up in the morning, we rack our brains trying to remember an important errand we need to run. But once we capture that item on a list on some sort of CPA (Comprehensive Personal Agenda), we get it off our minds and onto paper; and then we process it each morning and give thought to our steps.

Ask yourself, *What is the simplest way for me to keep track of my priorities and tasks?* You may be unable to keep up with too many categories or too much complication. But, whether with keypad, touchpad, or pen and ink, a little list will keep your ship from listing as you sail through the day.

Study Questions for Mastering This Pattern

1. When you look at the organization embedded in God's creation, what most amazes you?

_____

_____

_____

_____

2. Would you describe yourself as well organized? Why or why not?

_____

_____

_____

_____

3. What areas of your life could be better ordered?

_____

_____

_____

_____

4. If you were an organizational consultant advising yourself about your own life, what first practical steps would you suggest taking?

_____

_____

_____

_____

For more help in applying these principles or for group study or staff training, download my free _Mastering Life Workbook_ at RobertJMorgan.com/MasteringLifeWorkbook.

THE FOURTH PATTERN

Maximize the Morning

The first hour in the morning is the rudder of the day.

—Henry Ward Beecher[1]

11

Awake, My Soul, and with the Sun

Recently, while visiting New York City, I rose each morning about six and walked a few blocks to a little coffee shop on the Upper West Side. There each day I found a table, got my coffee and muffin, and enjoyed my morning routine of Bible study and prayer. I also silently studied the other customers and noticed an old fellow who came at about the same hour each morning. He was elderly, a little overweight, scruffy, with gray, uncombed hair and age spots, wearing a stocking hat and a scarf. His sweater had a hole in the shoulder. After getting two cookies and a cup of coffee, he sat down at the table in the window, muttered something to himself (maybe he was saying grace), and pulled a paperback from his shirt pocket. He read his novel for about twenty minutes, sipping his coffee and nibbling his cookies. Then he shoved his book back into his pocket, reassembled his cap and scarf, and left. His routine never varied.

One morning I got there before he did and took his table. When he came in, I saw him glance in my direction, none too happy, as he went to the counter to order his coffee. I didn't have the heart to disrupt his pattern, so while his back was turned I changed tables. Getting his breakfast, the old fellow shuffled over to his regular spot and settled into his usual routine, which, I suppose, characterized practically every day of his life. *Our lives are probably very different*, I thought, *but they're alike in this—we need our morning routine.*

Everyone has a morning protocol of some sort, and our morning rituals are like magnets bending the arc of our whole day. They go a long way toward defining who we are and determining the demeanor of our unfolding hours. If we complete an average life span, we'll greet more than twenty-five thousand mornings. Because God created the universe using circles and circuits and orbits, we have continual sets of new beginnings—a new day every twenty-four hours as the world spins on its axis, and a new year every 365 days as the planet orbits the sun. Each new day is a new start, a fresh little segment of life reborn. How we begin the morning determines whether we'll be pleasant and productive throughout the day. The early hours are the prologue to day and to the pristine liturgy of life.

In olden times, church hymnals were divided into topical segments and several pages were often devoted to "morning hymns." For example, the Doxology, one of our oldest English hymns, was written in 1674 as the chorus or refrain to a morning hymn written by Thomas Ken, who was an educational leader at Winchester College. At the time, hymn singing was frowned upon in churches but often used in private devotions.[2] Ken wanted his scholars to start each day with an attitude of praise, so he wrote a personal hymn for them:

Awake, my soul, and with the sun
Thy daily stage of duty run;
Shake off dull sloth, and joyful rise,
To pay thy morning sacrifice.

Direct, control, suggest this day,
All I design, or do, or say,
That all my powers, with all their might,
In Thy sole glory may unite.

Praise God, from whom all blessings flow;
Praise Him, all creatures here below;
Praise Him above, ye heavenly host;
Praise Father, Son, and Holy Ghost.

The most important thing about our day is beginning it with a spirit of doxology. If we get started on the right foot, we'll be ahead of the game all day long. The heroes of the Bible certainly knew this. In the Sinai wilderness, the Israelites went out and gathered manna for nourishment each morning (Exodus 16:21). When the tabernacle was set up, Aaron was told to burn fragrant incense on the altar every morning when he tended the lamps (Exodus 30:7). The priests were to begin each day with the morning sacrifices (Leviticus 6:12).

When King David established the regular worship patterns in the capital city of Jerusalem, he decreed that each day should begin with the Levitical choirs singing and thanking and praising God (1 Chronicles 23:30).

The patriarch Job began the day by offering sacrifices early in the morning for his family (Job 1:5).

The psalmist said, "In the morning, O Lord, you hear my voice; in the morning I lay my requests before you and wait in expectation" (Psalm 5:3).

The author of Psalm 59:16 wrote, "I will sing of your strength, in the morning I will sing of your love; for you are my fortress." In Psalm 88:13, he prayed, "In the morning my prayer comes before you."

Moses prayed in Psalm 90:14, "Satisfy us in the morning with your unfailing love, that we may sing for joy and be glad all our days."

The prophet Ezekiel said, "In the morning the word of the Lord came to me" (Ezekiel 12:8).

The greatest event in history occurred as the sun was rising over

Jerusalem and a faithful band of women trekked to the garden tomb, which they found empty. It was a great day in the morning, the greatest day that ever was.

The Bible's premier example of starting the day is given in a simple verse in Mark 1:35: "Very early in the morning, while it was still dark, Jesus got up, left the house and went off to a solitary place, where he prayed."

The setting for Mark 1:35 is the town of Capernaum, where Jesus was staying in the home of Simon Peter. I've visited the ruins of Capernaum many times, and it's easy to visualize the silent, solitary figure of the Lord Jesus, dressing warmly in the darkness, slipping through the shadows, out of the small town, across the road called the Via Maris, and onto a nearby mountainside where he could pray while watching the sun rise over the Golan Heights and pour its golden rays onto the choppy waters of the Sea of Galilee.

It is supremely biblical to begin each day with a sacred ritual, a spiritual routine, one that includes a standing appointment with the Lord to hear His voice, seek His blessings, and get His agenda for the day.

This is the intent of Psalm 143:8, in which David wrote: "Let the morning bring me word of your unfailing love, for I have put my trust in you. Show me the way I should go." In other words, "Lord, let me have a meeting with You every morning to look in the Book that tells me of Your unfailing love, to reaffirm my trust in You, and to seek Your blessings for the day ahead and Your guidance on the way I should go."

One of my favorite writers, the Salvation Army pioneer Samuel Logan Brengle, put it like this:

> If you would redeem the time, begin the moment your eyes open in the morning. Let no idle, foolish, hurtful thoughts be harbored for an instant, but begin at once to pray and

praise God and to meditate on His glories, His goodness and faithfulness and truth, and your heart will soon burn within you and bubble over with joy. Bounce out of your bed at once and get the start of your work and push it, else it will get the start and push you. For if you in the morning throw the minutes away, you can't pick them up in the course of the day.[3]

When I was in college, the campus radio station came on the air each morning at 6:15. I had my radio clock set to it, and the station began each morning with the same song—an old German Catholic hymn that became one of my favorites. The uplifting musical tune, "*Laudes Domini*," dates from 1868. I still often think of this hymn upon rising in the morning, and I'd like to share it with you in closing out this chapter.

> *When morning gilds the skies my heart awaking cries:*
> *May Jesus Christ be praised!*
> *Alike at work and prayer, to Jesus I repair:*
> *May Jesus Christ be praised!*
>
> *When you begin the day, O never fail to say,*
> *May Jesus Christ be praised!*
> *And at your work rejoice, to sing with heart and voice,*
> *May Jesus Christ be praised!*[4]

In the morning my spirit longs for you . . .
Be our strength every morning . . .
The Sovereign Lord has given me an instructed tongue,
to know the word that sustains the weary.
He wakens me morning by morning,
wakens my ear to listen like one being taught.

—Isaiah 26:9, 33:2, 50:4

12

Our First Appointment Each Day

When the president of the United States arrives in the West Wing each morning, the Presidential Daily Briefing is lying on the Oval Office desk. The PDB is usually about fifteen pages long and accompanied by a visit from a high-ranking official such as the director of the Central Intelligence Agency, who provides face-to-face insights. The PDB, a practice dating to the Truman administration, is vital for presidential leadership and for the security and stability of the world. When George W. Bush was elected to the White House, his father, former president George H. W. Bush, told him to never miss these top-of-the-morning meetings, for they are the most important part of the president's day.

That's exactly how I feel when I start each morning with a Bible on my desk and an accompanying daily appointment with the Lord: My morning devotions are vital to my state of mind as I prepare for the day. Everyone's schedule is different; our obligations in life vary from person to person. Your "morning devotions" might happen during the lunch hour, at bedtime, or at some other regular spot on your daily agenda. We have to be creative in planning our quiet times when we have young children, stressful obligations, or tough schedules. The timing is flexible, but the habit isn't—though a lot of Christians seem to think otherwise. I frequently ask people in my church if they have a regular time of daily Bible reading and prayer. I get a lot of "try to" answers. I don't really understand that. We either do it or we don't.

If we do, we're unusually blessed, for the Bible says, "Blessed is the man who listens to me, watching daily at my doors, waiting at my doorway" (Proverbs 8:34).

Between the covers of our Bibles we have access to a document more accurate and life altering than any prepared for a head of state. It's more relevant to our needs than any summary of the news, and more encouraging than any top-secret file. It provides more wisdom than any intelligence report. And, just like the Presidential Daily Briefing, the written message is accompanied by someone who sits down with us to help us understand it. As we sit at the kitchen table and pour over God's Word, the Lord Himself comes to meet with us. This is a prime opportunity to do what Brother Lawrence called "practice the presence of God."[1]

In his Sermon on the Mount, Jesus said, "When you pray, go into your room, close the door and pray to your Father, who is unseen. Then your Father, who sees what is done in secret, will reward you" (Matthew 6:6).

Do not have your concert first, and then tune your instrument afterwards. Begin the day with the Word of God and prayer, and get first of all into harmony with Him.

—**Missionary J. Hudson Taylor**[2]

This practice goes by many names: daily devotions, morning devotions, morning watch, quiet time—but you can think of it as the first appointment of the day, or a divine appointment. My dad taught me to read the Bible every night in bed, so I acquired that habit when I was old enough to read. But my morning quiet time habit started in the fall of 1971, thanks to the advice of some very good mentors.

In the decades since, my morning appointment has been the anchor of every day. We all need our diversions, but we need our devotions more. If I miss my time with the Lord, I go through the day feeling something is missing, so I try never to miss a morning, and certainly never to miss two in a row. Whether at home or traveling, whether working or on vacation, I don't want to neglect my regular meeting with the Lord. I agree with the Puritan Stephen Charnock, who said that even if the foundations of the world were ripped up and the heavens clattered and collapsed, we can maintain stability in our lives because our stability doesn't depend on the uncertain times but on the unchangeable rock of the truth of God.[3]

In its essence, our daily devotions represent a personal appointment with our Father and Friend, in which we converse with Him— talk to Him in prayer and listen to Him by reading and meditating on His Word. The core of daily devotions is a living friendship with Almighty God, which Christ provided through His death and resurrection.

In terms of technique, everyone develops his or her daily devotional habits a little differently, just as all our friendships have their own unique patterns. For the sake of practicality, I'll tell you how I go about it, but you'll enjoy developing your own pattern. Each morning, after I rise and shower and have a light breakfast, I sit down at the walnut desk my uncle Tom Morgan, a woodcrafter, made for me when I was a child. On the adjacent windowsill are a couple of study Bibles, a hymnbook, and a small selection of devotional books.

When I'm traveling, a hotel room does nicely. If I'm not alone in the room, I'll slip out to a poolside table or nearby coffee shop.

Sometimes it's nice to find a secluded mountain vista or park bench, or to walk along the beach. A friend told me about a man who lived in a small house with four children. The garage housed a furnace, a hot water heater, and miscellaneous equipment. This man had nailed up some plywood and made a small room with a door, about the size of a phone booth. There he had a little chair, a light, and a shelf for his Bible and prayer lists, and there he met each morning with the Creator of the universe.

Whether I'm at my upstairs desk, at a scenic overlook, or in the corner of a garage, I practice a similar routine. I usually begin the appointment with some simple journaling, jotting the date, a few notes about the day before or the one just beginning, and listing the passage I'm coming to in my daily Bible reading. Offering a quick prayer asking the Lord to speak to me in His Word, I open my Bible to where I left off the day before. I'm in no hurry to rush through a passage, so I may spend several days in the same paragraph. On other days I might read several chapters. My goal is finding some spiritual nourishment for the day, some verse that speaks to me. I'll often make a few notes or copy the verse into my journal, or turn the passage into a prayer I jot down.

Sometimes I spend the time memorizing the passage. Earlier this year, for example, I devoted quite a few days to Psalm 150 with the goal of memorizing all six verses. When we memorize passages, the Word of God sinks into our subconscious and allows the Holy Spirit to work around the clock in the deepest regions of our hearts and minds.[4]

Occasionally I've worked through the Bible, Genesis to Revelation, but usually I just choose a book at a time. Right now I'm working my way through Ezra. Though I'm a preacher, I don't use this time to look for sermon outlines, yet somehow I often end up teaching from the passages that have spoken to me during my quiet time.

After ten to thirty minutes of meditating on God's Word, I turn my focus to prayer. It helps to visualize the Lord Jesus close at hand and to talk to Him as if He were really there—which, of course, He is. Because this is a relationship more than a routine or ritual, I don't want to make it too perfunctory. But in keeping with what I said earlier about the utility of listing things, I do find prayer lists helpful. I have a number of them in my journal—for personal needs, for family members, for missionaries, for prodigals, for any number of other things. I don't cover every item every day, but I talk with the Lord about what's most on my heart, using my lists to keep me from forgetting to pray often for those things that represent my "daily bread." In time, these prayer lists become praise lists and serve as an ongoing record of answered prayer.

Having spent time in the Word and in conversing with the Lord, I often conclude my appointment by reading from an inspirational book or by singing or reading the words to a hymn.

At the end of the day, my work behind me, I frequently repeat the process in briefer fashion and often recite the Lord's Prayer before falling asleep. Prayer truly is, as it's been said, the key to the morning and the bolt of the evening.

Our divine appointment with the Lord encapsulates our daily walk with God. Of course, we walk with the Lord throughout the day and practice His presence through all our waking moments. The Lord is constantly with His children. As we draw near to Him, He draws near to us, and we can offer spontaneous prayers at any moment, silently or aloud. We mustn't segregate our sacred time from our secular lives. My point is, we're aided in our daily walk if we get it started on the right foot each morning.

Don't just take my word for it. Whenever we read biographies of great Christians from any era of history, we find they practiced this habit faithfully. It's always been the secret of pleasantly productive people.[5]

Missionary Bertha Smith, for example, wrote a fascinating autobiography in which she told about her determination to keep the divine appointment each day. It was bitterly cold in her part of China. During the day she wore thirty pounds of clothing, and at night she slept with a hot water bottle under heavy bedding. But her challenge came in the early morning, when she wanted to rise before others so she could have her quiet time before the scores of interruptions each day brought. She would struggle in the darkness to put on her layers of clothing and break the ice to wash her face in cold water. Then she slipped out to a particular haystack where she raked aside the frosted part of the hay, knelt down, and spent time with the Lord before the sun came up.[6]

William Carey, the Father of Modern Missions, served many years in the land of Burma, and this is the habit that sustained him. His biographer wrote,

> In the walled garden of the mission house at Serampore, he built an arbor which he called his "bower." There at sunrise, before tea, and at the time of full moon when there was the least danger from snakes, he meditated and prayed, and the Book which he ceaselessly translated for others was his own source of strength and refreshment.[7]

Thomas Watson summed it up with typical Puritan sagacity when he wrote: "The best time to converse with God is before worldly occasions stand knocking at the door to be let in: The morning is, as it were, the cream of the day, let the cream be taken off, and let God have it. Wind up thy heart towards heaven at the beginning of the day, and it will go the better all the day after."[8]

George Muller, renowned for his vast prayer-based ministry of orphan care, became as close to an expert in daily devotions as anyone. His insights have influenced how I have my quiet time today. Listen to his testimony about his daily appointment:

The first great and primary business to which I ought to attend every day was, to have my soul happy in the Lord. The first thing to be concerned about was not how much I might serve the Lord, how I might glorify the Lord; but how I might get my soul into a happy state, and how my inner man might be nourished. . . .

Before this time my practice had been, at least for ten years previously, as a habitual thing, to give myself to prayer after having dressed myself in the morning. Now, I saw that the most important . . . was to give myself to the reading of the Word of God, and to meditation on it, that thus my heart might be comforted, encouraged, warned, reproved, instructed. . . .

The first thing I did, after having asked in a few words the Lord's blessing upon his precious Word, was to begin to meditate on the Word of God, searching as it were into every verse to get blessing out of it; not for the sake of public ministry of the Word . . . but for the sake of obtaining food for my soul.

The result I have found to be almost invariably this, that after a very few minutes my soul has been led to confession, or to thanksgiving, or to supplication; so that, though I did not, as it were, give myself to prayer, but to meditation, yet it turned almost immediately more or less into prayer. . . .

By breakfast time, with rare exceptions, I am in a peaceful if not happy state of heart.[9]

The Lord is more concerned about our *walk with Him* than our *work for Him*. Don't miss another day of fellowship with the Father. Start first thing in the morning, which means making some preparations tonight. Plan ahead. Find a place. Set out your coffee mug. Go out and buy a simple notebook or find an online journaling tool. Open your Bible to the spot you want to read. Set your alarm clock if you need so, and go to bed a little earlier.

In the morning, you have an appointment to keep. The God of the universe will be waiting on you, so don't be late.

> *He who every morning plans the transaction of the day and follows out the plan, carries a thread that will guide him through the labyrinth of the most busy life.*
>
> —Hugh Blair, eighteenth-century Scottish clergyman[1]

13

Before Leaving the Presence

The Bible says, "Do not be in a hurry to leave the king's presence" (Ecclesiastes 8:3). In that spirit, I want to suggest a technique to tie together all the strands of the prior pages of *Mastering Life Before It's Too Late*. So far we've talked about starting each day committed to our Father's business. We've discussed the worth of time and being organized enough to redeem it. We've examined the utility of calendars and planning and lists. And we've reviewed the greatest moment of the day—our daily appointment with God. Simple concepts, really, but so underutilized and life changing. They require a smattering of discipline and a bundle of grace. Is there a simple scheme for doing it all?

Here is the best system I've found for making sense of every day. Before I leave the conscious presence of God at the end of my morning quiet time, I take a few moments to look prayerfully at my lists of obligations and my calendar. On a little four-by-six card, I scratch out a plan. You can do this on an electronic device, of course. I use a card because I stick it in my pocket and carry it with me all day.

After briefly considering my priorities and agenda, I jot at the top of that card the one thing I most need to accomplish that day. Perhaps there are two or three things, but almost never more than three. I draw a box around them. In the space beneath I jot down anything else I need to remember about the day—perhaps a list of my appointments or other to-do items I should tackle if possible. On the back of the card, I usually write my current Bible memory verse.

That becomes my plan for the day.

In just two or three minutes, at the end of your morning devotion and as you segue from the mountaintop to the workplace or classroom, you can devise a blueprint for the hours before you. This harkens back to a verse I mentioned earlier—Psalm 143:8: "Let the morning bring me word of your unfailing love, for I have put my trust in you. Show me the way I should go."

In other words, "Lord, this morning remind me of Your love and show me Your agenda for today."

The most productive leaders in the world of business and commerce practice a secular version of this without fail. In his book on efficiency, *Eat That Frog,* Brian Tracy wrote, "It takes only about 10 to 12 minutes for you to plan out your day, but this small investment of time will save you up to two hours (100 to 120 minutes) in wasted time and diffused effort throughout your day."[2]

Tracy explained, "Throughout my career, I have discovered and rediscovered a simple truth. The ability to concentrate single-mindedly on your most important task, to do it well and to finish it completely, is the key to great success, achievement, respect, status, and happiness in life."[3] He continued, "An average person who develops the habit of setting clear priorities and getting important tasks completed quickly will run circles around a genius who talks a lot and makes wonderful plans but who gets very little done."[4]

In the history of business and management literature, this concept is often first credited to Ivy Ledbetter Lee, the son of a Methodist minister, who helped establish the field of public relations. In that capacity, he worked as an adviser for Bethlehem Steel Corporation. Mr. Lee coached his clients to develop a simple scheme of listing and numbering their top priorities each day so they could concentrate their energy on completing their daily list, a task at a time, in order of importance.

One day the president of Bethlehem Steel, Charles Michael Schwab, asked Lee, "Show me a way to get more things done with my time and I'll pay you any fee within reason." Handing Schwab a blank sheet of paper, Ivy Lee said,

> Write down the most important tasks you have to do to-morrow and number them in order of importance. When you arrive in the morning, begin at once on Number One and stay on it till it's completed. Recheck your priorities; then begin with Number Two. If any task takes all day, never mind. Stick with it as long as it's the most important one. If you don't finish them all, you probably couldn't do so with any other method, and without some system you'd proba-bly not even decide which one was most important. Make this a habit every working day. When it works for you, give it to your men. Try it as long as you like. Then send me your check for what you think it's worth.[5]

Schwab later sent Lee a check for $25,000, a colossal sum in those days, saying the lesson was the most practical and profound he had ever discovered in his professional life. Within five years, this plan was largely responsible for turning Bethlehem Steel into the biggest independent steel producer in the world, and it helped turn Charles M. Schwab into one of the richest men on earth.[6]

I can't guarantee that Lee's methods will make you rich and fa-mous, but I'm sure you'll become more pleasantly productive if you devise a version of this system and correlate it with your daily ap-pointment. It's the simplest way possible to arrange your tasks, track your duties, prioritize your time, and tackle life one project at a time. Get organized and give thought to your steps. Ask the God who gives us His helpful lists to keep you from being listless. He can enable you to order your days, arrange your work, and fulfill His will, one blessed task at a time.

Remember the biblical maxim: "One thing I do."

In the morning, with its freshness and quiet, the believer can look out upon the day. He can consider its duties and its temptations, and pass them through beforehand, as it were, with his Savior.

—Andrew Murray[7]

There's another benefit to having a plan for the day: it helps us deal with those dreaded interruptions that can shred our best-made plans like razors. After all, after meeting with the Lord, lingering in His presence, and devising a plan, we launch into uncharted waters. None of us knows what a day will bring. But we can better handle interruptions *with* a plan than *without* one. If you have no personal agenda at all, you'll be fully at the mercy of interruptions. When you have an agenda, you can minimize the interruptions and accept the unavoidable ones as from the Lord.

Sometimes the interruptions represent the Father's business, as we learn by studying the life of Christ. He met with the Father every day and lived on a strict personal schedule. But sometimes the interruptions became His ministry, such as the time four men disrupted His sermon by breaking through the roof above Him and lowering their friend down on a mat for healing. Or the time a bleeding woman touched the hem of His garment. Or the time Thomas broke into His discourse and said, "Lord, we don't know where you are going, so how can we know the way?" That occasioned one of Christ's most famous statements: "I am the way and the truth and the life" (John 14:6).

I use my personal daily agenda to focus on the most important tasks of each day, trying to avoid the tyranny of the urgent. But when, despite my best efforts, interruptions occur, I try to respond in a relaxed way (I'm not always successful!), remembering that interruptions can be God's way of showing us our next assignment.

The days aren't easy, but the plan is simple. As you meet with the Lord each morning, don't leave His presence without asking for His tasks for the day and His blessings on your life and work. In prayer, give thought to your steps. It's the best way I've found to be about the Father's business.

Get into the habit of dealing with God about everything.
Unless you learn to open the door of your life completely
and let God in from your first waking moment of each new day,
you will be working on the wrong level throughout the day.
But if you will swing the door of your life fully open
and pray to your Father who is in the secret place,
every public thing in your life will be marked
with the lasting imprint of the presence of God.

—Oswald Chambers[1]

14

Try the Fifteen-Minute Plan

If you're so overwhelmed you can't conceive of taking time for a daily appointment of leisurely Bible study, prayer, and planning, then start small. Try a dedicated fifteen minutes. In round figures, that amounts to about a hundred minutes out of the ten thousand allotted by God for each week—only 1 percent of your time. That might be the best you can manage if you're just beginning to master life, but be encouraged. That's a good start.

Sometime ago I had to take a quick trip to St. Louis, so I asked a buddy to go with me. I've known this young man since he was a boy and have always appreciated him. But until that trip, I had no idea of the daily pressures he faced. Driving through the night, he told me of the demands on him. His marriage was two years old, and a child was on the way. He was trying to stay involved in church, but the financial stresses of starting his own business had overtaken his schedule. The economy was bad, so from early in the morning until late at night, he was out meeting clients, balancing books, producing results, and making things happen. He was also trying to be a good husband and preparing to be a good dad.

As we talked about time management and daily devotions, it seemed to intimidate him. He didn't have *time* to manage his *time*. The ideas I've written about in this book, as simple as they are, seemed beyond his reach. He reminded me of the little boy running down the road pushing his bicycle. When someone asked him why he wasn't riding the thing, he yelled back, "I'm so late I don't have time to get on it."

I told my friend that story, then said, "I want you to try something. I'm confident that somehow in the course of twenty-four hours you can find fifteen minutes for yourself, just a quarter hour. Using your wristwatch, I want you to read your Bible for five minutes, pray for five minutes, and use the last five minutes to plan out your day. It sounds legalistic, but try this consistently for one month. Keep the time uninterrupted and then tell me how it works."

He started the next morning. Sitting at his kitchen table and knowing he had an uninterrupted fifteen minutes, he didn't feel rushed. He read from the book of Proverbs for five minutes, taking his time from verse to verse. Then he prayed for a solid five minutes. Then he took his calendar and "to do" list and sketched out a plan for the day, using the full five minutes to think things through.

"I've been doing what you suggested," he told me a month later. "It's worked! I feel better connected with the Lord, more at peace with myself, and more in charge of my day. I can't believe the difference a quarter hour can make."

Remember what we said in an earlier chapter about the power of fifteen-minute segments of time? God can do more with fifteen minutes than we can accomplish in a lifetime. To Him, a day is like a thousand years and a thousand years like a day. When He plans our hours, He always leaves some time for Himself. When He's in control of our schedules, we'll be able to abide in Him, for He cannot neglect himself.

If the pressures of life are getting the best of you, set aside a quarter hour and see what God can do with it. When you start the day on the right foot, you'll seldom go wrong.

Study Questions for Mastering This Pattern

1. Describe your morning routine.

_____

_____

_____

_____

2. Is it realistic for you to establish a better morning routine, or is some other time of the day better for finding the quietness needed to still and stabilize your heart and mind?

_____

_____

_____

_____

3. Do you have a daily appointment? Why or why not?

_____

_____

_____

_____

4. Is the fifteen-minute plan viable for you? How can you foresee developing your own daily appointment habits?

_____

_____

_____

_____

For more help in applying these principles or for group study or staff training, download my free _Mastering Life Workbook_ at RobertJMorgan.com/MasteringLifeWorkbook.

THE FIFTH PATTERN

Pull Off at Rest Stops

It is senseless for you to work so hard from
early morning until late at night,
fearing you will starve to death;
for God wants his loved ones to get their proper rest.

—Psalm 127:2[1]

15

Make Wise Withdrawals

Quick—who said these words: "Get some rest!"?

Believe it or not, that simple sentence is a red-letter commandment from the lips of the Son of God, as recorded word for word in Mark 6:31. I added the exclamation mark, but only because Mark was writing in the Greek language, which didn't use punctuation. I'm sure Jesus spoke with insistency, because the words were directed at His disciples, who were nearing exhaustion following the miraculous feeding of the multitudes on the slopes above Lake Galilee. Because so many people were incessantly coming and going, the Twelve hadn't had a chance to eat. They were spent. So Jesus told them, "Come with me by yourselves to a quiet place and *get some rest.*"

These last three words may be the most important ones you read in this book. It's not just a three-syllable statement spoken by Jesus in Mark 6:31; it's a consistent teaching throughout Scripture, established at the Creation when God sanctioned the Sabbath as the ultimate example of resting amid our work. God didn't create humans to run like robots. We have limited reservoirs of energy, and we require frequent periods of rest—mental, physical, and spiritual intermissions—to replenish our resources.

So far in *Mastering Life,* I've taken an aggressive approach to finding God's will, going about the Father's business, redeeming the time, staying self-disciplined and well organized, maximizing each morning for the Lord's glory, and seeking to complete God's plan for each day. If the prior chapters sounded as if they were written by a workaholic, well, maybe they were; but I'm certain God doesn't want us to live in a state of chronic exhaustion. If we're always tired, something's wrong. If we live in perpetual fatigue, it's time to bring a new rhythm into our hours, days, and weeks.

A single letter separates the words *business* and *busyness*, but there's an immense chasm between the two concepts. Jesus had to be about His Father's *business*, but He said nothing of His Father's *busyness*. Despite having only thirty-three years to invest on earth— only three of which were spent in vocational ministry—our Lord never displayed a windmill-in-a-storm visage. His agenda never deteriorated into spinning, frenetic activity. He never appeared hurried or harried. He was often tired—once He fell asleep during a storm at sea—but He knew how to renew His strength and restore His stamina through rest and withdrawal.

Busyness is like the con man your aunt Josephine married. Perhaps he can't always be avoided, but he should be viewed warily. *Busyness* sneaks up on you, makes you think you're more important than you are, and sells you a set of activities that are usually overvalued. Someone said, "If the devil can't make you bad, he'll make you busy." That's often true, so we must beware the barrenness of busyness.

Personally, I like to stay busy. Most of us do; but there are two caveats. First, we have to be busy doing the right things. As American writer Mary O'Connor put it, "It's not so much how busy you are, but why you are busy. The bee is praised. The mosquito is swatted."[2]

Second, we have to guard against staying *too* busy. Some people burn their candles at both ends; others burn their ends at both candles. In either case, the light goes out. The old proverb about burning candles is usually misunderstood. When we say we're burning our candles at both ends, we don't mean both ends of the *candle* but both ends of the *day*. We wake up too early and have to light our candles till the sun comes up; and later when the sun retires we have to light our candles again to work into the night. Too many days like that, and we'll burn out both our candles and ourselves. Constant activity frays our nerves, agitates our minds, drains us spiritually, plunders us emotionally, and debilitates us physically.

In her devotional classic *Springs in the Valley*, Mrs. Charles M. Cowman wrote, "Many are slowly succumbing to the strain of life because they have forgotten how to rest. . . . Rest is not a sedative for the sick, but a tonic for the strong. . . . It saves us from becoming slaves even of good works."[3]

There's never a reason to waste time, but we aren't wasting time when we're recharging our batteries and restocking our hearts. We need time to think. To meditate. To study interesting subjects in the Bible. To memorize helpful passages. To pray through things. To divert ourselves with the wonders of creation. To withdraw. To walk. To sleep. To read to our children. To jog on the beach, splash in the waves, hike in the mountains, or swing in the hammock. Time to sleep. Time to withdraw from the worry.

This is a crucial difference between Christians and everyone else on the planet. Most of the world works hard so they can enjoy their leisure. Christians enjoy their leisure so they can work hard. That's not just a turn of a phrase; it's a totally different perspective on life.

Jesus Himself embodied this attitude. Some time ago I read through the Gospels, looking for every occasion when our Lord Jesus "withdrew." I noticed that despite the short, three-year nature of His intense work, He had a way of dropping off the radar screen when He wanted or needed to. He understood a basic principle of life: If you're always available, you're never available.

The following list of verses is long, but I want to impress you with the sheer preponderance of this habit in Jesus' life. Don't skip over them. Read each one in turn, and notice how frequently the Bible shows us this habit in the Lord's routine:

- Then Jesus was led by the Spirit into the wilderness . . . forty days and forty nights. (Matthew 4:1)

- Very early in the morning, while it was still dark, Jesus got up, left the house and went off to a solitary place, where he prayed. Simon and his companions went to look for him, and when they found him, they exclaimed, "Everyone is looking for you!" (Mark 1:35–37)

- At daybreak, Jesus went out to a solitary place. The people were looking for him. (Luke 4:42)

- One of those days Jesus went out to a mountainside to pray, and spent the night praying to God. (Luke 6:12)

- When Jesus heard what had happened, he withdrew by boat privately to a solitary place. (Matthew 14:13)

- Jesus often withdrew to lonely places and prayed. (Luke 5:16)

- Jesus withdrew with his disciples to the lake. (Mark 3:7)

- Come with me by yourselves to a quiet place. (Mark 6:31)

- When the apostles returned, they reported to Jesus what they had done. Then he took them with him and they withdrew by themselves. (Luke 9:10)

- Immediately Jesus made the disciples get into the boat and go on ahead of him to the other side, while he dismissed the crowd. After he had dismissed them, he went up on a mountainside by himself to pray. Later that night, he was there alone. (Matthew 14:22–23)

- Jesus, knowing that they intended to come and make him king by force, withdrew again to a mountain by himself. (John 6:15)

- Then they all went home, but Jesus went to the Mount of Olives. (John 7:53)

- Jesus left that place and went to the vicinity of Tyre. He entered a house and did not want anyone to know it. (Mark 7:24)

- Jesus took with him Peter, James, and John the brother of James, and led them up on a high mountain by themselves. (Matthew 17:1)

- They left that place and passed through Galilee. Jesus did not want anyone to know where they were. (Mark 9:30)

- Then Jesus went back across the Jordan to the place where John had been baptizing in the early days. There he stayed. (John 10:40)

- Jesus no longer moved about publicly among the people of Judea. Instead he withdrew to a region near the wilderness. (John 11:54)

- When he had finished speaking, Jesus left and hid himself from them. (John 12:36)

- Leaving there, he went, as he so often did, to Mount Olives. (Luke 22:39)

- He withdrew. (Luke 22:41)

Only three brief years, yet how often our Lord was unavailable! He measured out His strength for each task, replenished His soul at frequent intervals, rested in mind and body as necessary, and guarded against physical breakdowns and emotional burnout.

If we're going to finish the work God has given us, we must learn to make wise withdrawals. We need interruptions from the stress, with shorter breaks during shorter times and longer breaks during longer times. We need getaway moments, getaway hours, and getaway days. We need adequate sleep at night, for sleep deprivation is the curse of our age.

I'm writing these words on New Year's Day, and in this morning's news was a piece suggesting the most important New Year's resolution for most people might involve sleep. Arranging our schedule to get a little more sleep at night would do more than anything else, suggested the article, to help us lose weight, be sharper, stay happier, and live longer. "Improving sleep during the nighttime can really be very effective in improving quality of life in the daytime," said one expert quoted in the article.[4]

Some years ago, I experienced a difficult period of stress with a small group of people. I'm partly to blame. It started when one of them came to me with a strong opinion about something, and I made the mistake of meeting him while tired. Instead of responding wisely, I overreacted. My words were a little sharper and more adamant than they should have been. My questioner took great offense and could never get over it. Perhaps he was overworked and overwrought too. Matters went from bad to worse, and they still haven't been resolved to my satisfaction. I can't blame everything on fatigue, but being overtaxed didn't help.

When my children were young, I could always tell when they were tired. Their grip on their emotions weakened, and the best thing I could do during their meltdowns was try to get them to give up and go to bed. When my eldest daughter was a teenager, I always knew when she was tired; she was prone to fits of disconsolate weeping over little things, though in her run-down state they didn't seem small to her. "Just go to bed," I would tell her. "It's not as bad as all that; you're just tired." She never appreciated the advice, but it was the truth. And now, today, the same is true for you and me when we let ourselves get worn out. We have less ability to manage our emotions, guard our reactions, and maintain healthy attitudes.

If you want to be a pleasantly productive person, take seriously the words of Jesus in Mark 6:31: "Get some rest!"

Never be in a hurry; do everything quietly and in a calm spirit.
Do not lose your inward peace for anything whatsoever,
even if your whole world seems upset.
When does anything belonging to this life matter,
when compared with a peaceful heart?
Commend all to God, and then lie still
and be at rest in His bosom.
Whatever happens, abide steadfast in a determination to cling
simply to God, trusting in His Eternal Love for you . . .
Maintain a holy simplicity of mind,
and do not smother yourself with a host of cares,
wishes, or longings, under any pretext.

—Saint Francis de Sales, in a letter to Madame de Chantal[1]

16

Take Heed to Yourself

Robert Murray M'Cheyne was a famous Scottish pastor, one of the most powerful preachers ever to stand in the pulpits of Edinburgh and Dundee, but he died at age twenty-nine, partly because he had weakened his constitution by overwork, excessive busyness, and chronic fatigue. He reportedly said as he was dying, "The Lord gave me a horse to ride and a message to deliver. Alas, I have killed the horse and cannot deliver the message."[2]

I have a favorite Bible verse I frequently quote to tired people. It's the advice the apostle Paul gave to the church leaders in Ephesus in Acts 20:28: "Therefore take heed to yourselves and to all the flock, among which the Holy Spirit has made you overseers."[3] Notice the order of the sentence. We're to take heed to ourselves before we can take heed to the flock. If we don't take care of ourselves, we soon won't be able to take care of whatever flock or responsibility God has given us.

There's such a thing as a sanctified selfishness that isn't really selfish at all. When we take care of ourselves as God intended, it allows us to be a greater blessing to others in a richer way for a longer time. We have to keep the horse as healthy as possible so we can deliver the message as wisely and widely as the Lord commands.

Fatigue is counterproductive. It increases our inefficiency, shortens our tempers, stresses our schedules, makes our work heavier, and, if sustained over time, it can reduce our lives. Having a well-ordered life and taking advantage of every minute doesn't require living in a hyperkinetic frenzy. On the contrary, it allows us to build in times of stillness, solitude, green pastures, quiet waters, rest, thinking, family time, days off, needed vacations, hobbies, recreation, and relaxation.

The Bible calls this *rest*.

Biblical rest is the state of mind and body that allows God to restore our souls and replenish our strength. *Rest* is a divine idea. God Himself rested on the seventh day. He felt no fatigue and needed no restoration of strength, of course. His omnipotence is never diminished regardless of how much energy He expends. For God, *rest* was enjoying the interval between tasks completed and work to come. That's what it means to us too; but, being human, we also need the element of restored strength. Here's what the Bible says on the subject:

- The Lord replied, "My Presence will go with you, and I will give you rest." (Exodus 33:14)

- Six days you shall labor, but on the seventh day you shall rest; even during the plowing season and harvest you must rest. (Exodus 34:21)

- The ark of the covenant of the Lord went before them during those three days to find them a place to rest. (Numbers 10:33)

- The Lord gave them rest on every side. (Joshua 21:44)

- My soul finds rest in God. (Psalm 62:1)

- In repentance and rest is your salvation, in quietness and trust is your strength. (Isaiah 30:15)

- Ask for the ancient paths, ask where the good way is,
  and walk in it, and you will find rest for your souls.
  (Jeremiah 6:16)

- Take my yoke upon you and learn from me . . . and
  you will find rest for your souls. (Matthew 11:29)

- The promise of entering his rest still stands. (Hebrews
  4:1)

- Come with me by yourselves to a quiet place and get
  some rest. (Mark 6:31)

How do we *rest* in the biblical sense? There's a strong element of faith involved, for resting in the Lord is a *soul-rest* that means trusting Him with our trials and troubles. Psalm 37 says, "Trust in the Lord . . . feed on his faithfulness. . . . Rest in the Lord, and wait patiently for him; do not fret. . . ."[4] The apostle Paul said, "Therefore we do not lose heart. Though outwardly we are wasting away, yet inwardly we are being renewed day by day" (2 Corinthians 4:16).

But it's not just spiritual and mental; it's physical and emotional. Our bodies and souls are so intertwined, it's impossible to separate them. You can't abuse your body without hurting your soul; and you can't neglect your soul without damaging your body. Jesus called His people to double-rest. Twice He enjoined them to rest by using the same basic command: Come!

- Regarding rest of body, as we've seen in Mark 6:31, He
  said: "Come with me by yourselves to a quiet place
  and get some rest."

- Regarding rest of spirit, He said in Matthew 11:28–29:
  "Come to me, all you who are weary and burdened,
  and I will give you rest. Take my yoke upon you and

> learn from me, for I am gentle and humble in heart,
> and you will find rest for your souls."

Come. . . . Come. . . . It sounds simple, yet it was a hard lesson for me to grasp. For years I probably worked too hard. I'm not sure why, but I seldom took a day off except during family vacations; and I worked long days. I knew enough to guard my family times, and I cherished my wife and daughters. I also preserved my daily appointment with God, which kept me from burnout. But otherwise I was a driven man as it related to my work, and tired, and not always from the best motives. I sustained this pace for many years, but it finally caught up with me. Thankfully I didn't have a breakdown in body or spirit or home, but my frustration level reached a breaking point.

A friend and I traveled to France for a week or two, and I was in a state of exhaustion. I took two books with me—the Bible and Thoreau's *Walden*, with its appealing emphasis on the simple life. One day, sitting at a little outdoor café table waiting for a train, with both books open before me, I finally realized how exhausted I had become. If I didn't change, I realized, I would kill the horse.

On the spot, I opened my notebook and made a little list of corrective steps—taking a day off each week . . . not setting an alarm unless absolutely necessary . . . not working as late into the evenings . . . exercising more . . . taking Monday nights as an extra night off . . . leaving work early on Fridays . . . Things like that.

It was a turning point for me, and, looking back, those few moments beside a busy train station in Paris probably saved me from a breakdown. Not that the changes were easy to make. Though they were simple ideas, it took a long time for me to hammer them into my routine. But, knowing they were vital for the last half of my life, I worked hard to implement them, and I'm doing my best to stay true to them now. Because of those changes, I can say I'm often tired but seldom truly fatigued and almost never chronically exhausted. My friends, I think, will tell you I'm less irritable and more pleasantly productive.

For me, one of the most important steps involved a Sabbath—a day off. Since Sundays are workdays for me, I choose Saturday, the traditional Jewish Sabbath. I had a hard time trying to figure out what to do on a personal Sabbath day, but I finally made myself a simple rule: If it feels very much like work, I probably shouldn't do it on my day off. Everything else is permissible.

For workaholics, this is undeniably a form of self-denial, for Leviticus 16:29 says, regarding the Jewish festival days, "You must deny yourselves and do not do any work." We often work harder than we should because of fear ("I've got to keep the money coming in") or ambition ("I've got to succeed"). When we take a day off, we're denying ourselves the indulgences of fear and ambition, giving them to God and accepting His rest in return.

My friend Roy King advises, "Six days for work and one day for rest is very important to God. He ordered His own creative acts around that rhythm of producing and rest." In *Time Management Is Really Life Management,* King wrote:

> Rest is God's gift to you to replace what work takes out. One day of rest can replenish what six days of work takes out. In addition, God gave other work breaks to His people in the Bible called feasts and fasts. In some ways we have carried these breaks over into our experience today as retreats, holidays and vacations. God provides these rest places where we go to be replenished. Rest is a space that God gives us where we are removed from the expectations to be productive.[5]

Though I'm still living by the little set of rules I made for myself at the café table in Paris, I don't have a specific set of suggestions for you; you'll have to develop those yourself. But thinking them through, jotting them down, and following up on their implementation is the best way I know to "take heed to yourself" and keep the horse healthy.

When I enrolled in Columbia International University in 1971 and gave my life to the Lord, I signed up for a class taught by Dr. Otis Braswell, one of the godliest men I've ever met. The assigned text was *A Spiritual Clinic* by Dr. J. Oswald Sanders. As I read the book, I underlined these words, and now, years later, have come back to them:

> If we feel harassed and the pressure on us becomes too great, the time has arrived to take stock of our commitments and to resolutely refuse more than we can discharge well and without undue strain. By thus simplifying our living we shall be able for more, and may confidently count on the Holy Spirit to guide us in a path in which we shall neither selfishly save our lives nor foolishly overspend our nervous and spiritual capital. Such reorganization of living will demand stern self-discipline, but how well worthwhile.[6]

If we're going to be pleasantly productive people, we will frequently pull off at rest stops on the highway of life. Stillness and solitude are essential for the soul; and in quietness and confidence will be our strength. As the hymnist said:

> *Take time to be holy, the world rushes on;*
> *Spend much time in secret with Jesus alone.*
> *By looking to Jesus, like him thou shalt be;*
> *Thy friends in thy conduct his likeness shall see.*

Take time to be holy, be calm in thy soul,
Each thought and each motive beneath his control.
Thus led by his Spirit to foundations of love,
Thou soon shalt be fitted for service above.[7]

Why not take time out? What's the hurry?
We're passing through but once and we are
in such a dither to get from here to yonder
that we have not time to see anything on the way.
I am glad that I grew up in a quieter day
when we took time out in the hills
to watch the sun go down behind the mountains,
to sit on the porch at night and hear the whip-poor-will
or the dogs barking on a possum hunt far in the distance.
Life's tempo has picked up to a frantic pace since then,
but I have never lost entirely the training of my earlier days.
I may not be going as fast and I may not get as far,
but the boys who are passing me aren't too impressive.

—Vance Havner[1]

17

Only Do What Only You Can Do

To state the obvious: sometimes our fatigue comes from doing too much, which indicates we're piling the work of others atop the burdens we're already bearing. As we've seen, the Bible tells us, "The Lord has assigned to each his task" (1 Corinthians 3:5). When we're in the Lord's will, we find liberating happiness doing our God-assigned tasks, but there's little lasting joy in doing the work assigned to others. We need to offer them the blessing of reclaiming it for themselves. We need to say, "I love you, so I am not going to assume any of the work entrusted to you. In fact, here's some of my work that may be better fitted to your gifts and passions." In such transferals, we learn an important principle in mastering life—as much as it's possible, only do what only you can do.

This is as scriptural as it can be. In the Bible, the Lord created two great global enterprises. In the Old Testament, it was the nation of Israel. In the New Testament, the church. Early in the life of both organizations, we encounter this crucial principle of "Only do what only you can do."

In the case of Israel, look at what happened in the wilderness when Moses grew overwhelmed with his workload. In Exodus 18, he had a visit from his father-in-law and former employer, Jethro, who was a very astute businessman. Jethro observed Moses and evaluated his leadership strengths and weaknesses. Every day Moses took his seat as judge among the people, and long lines of unhappy souls queued up from morning till evening. They came to him one by one for his decisions regarding various issues. Jethro was exhausted just watching it, and after a while he pulled Moses aside and offered some advice as relevant today as then: "What you are doing is not good. You and these people who come to you will only wear yourselves out. The work is too heavy for you; you cannot handle it alone" (Exodus 18:17–18).

Imagine God speaking those words to you, personally and presently. Imagine Him saying to you as an administrator, as a pastor, as a volunteer, as a parent, as an executive in your company, or as an overinvolved student at your school: "You're working your hardest and trying your best. But what you are doing is not good. You'll only wear out yourself and others. The work is too heavy for you; you can't handle it alone."

Yes, but what do we do about it? Jethro advised Moses to select some qualified people, get them organized into a system, give them some training, and assign the work to them. Only the most difficult cases should come to Moses. "That will make your load lighter, because they will share it with you," Jethro said. "If you do this and God so commands, you will be able to stand the strain, and all these people will go home satisfied" (Exodus 18:22–23).

I nominate these words as the best business and management advice ever offered. The response was positive. Verse 24 reports, "Moses listened to his father-in-law and did everything as he said." This established the judicial system for ancient Israel and transferred much of Moses' authority to others, and with it his responsibilities. He learned to do only what he could do, because God had prepared others to do what he could not and should not do.

We find the New Testament parallel in Acts 6, when the first disagreement broke out in the early church. Some widows were being neglected in the distribution of benevolence. The apostles couldn't singlehandedly care of everyone's needs, so Peter convened a church meeting and said,

It would not be right for us to neglect the ministry of the Word of God in order to wait on tables. Brothers and sisters, choose seven men from among you who are known to be full of the Spirit and wisdom. We will turn this responsibility over to them and will give our attention to prayer and the ministry of the Word. (Acts 6:2–4)

They did exactly what Moses had done in Exodus 18. Looking back, we can say that without this strategic decision, the growth of the church would have been bottlenecked and hamstrung. But when the apostles, like Moses, learned to do what only they could do, "The word of God spread. The number of disciples in Jerusalem increased rapidly, and a large number of priests became obedient to the faith" (Acts 6:7).

Even Jesus Christ Himself—the most pleasantly productive person in history—lived by this rule. In Acts 10:38, the apostle Peter said Jesus was anointed with the Holy Spirit and "went around doing good." It doesn't say that He went around doing everything. Indeed, Jesus often left the scene while the work was seemingly unfinished. At the end of His three years of ministry, only a portion of a tiny nation had been reached. The world still overflowed with sick, lonely, dying people. His own region was dotted with towns and cities untouched by His message. But Jesus knew how to work Himself out of a job, so to speak. He was a master delegator, and He devoted much of His time to preparing a handful of people to take over His work, and through them to continue His cause.

We can clearly trace this habit through Matthew's Gospel. In Matthew 4, following His baptism by John and His temptation in the wilderness, Jesus officially began His ministry. If you consult a red-letter edition of the Bible, you can see two pronouncements that represent the first words Jesus spoke as He began His work. The first is in Matthew 4:17: "Repent, for the kingdom of heaven has come near." That was His core message. His second pronouncement was two verses later (verse 19), spoken to fishermen casting their nets into the lake. "Come, follow me," Jesus said, "and I will send you out to fish for people."

The first thing Jesus did was articulate His message. The second was delegate the work of spreading it.

The next chapter, Matthew 5, begins "Now when Jesus saw the crowds, He went up on a mountainside and sat down. His disciples came to Him, and He began to teach them" (Matthew 5:1–2). What follows is Christ's Sermon on the Mount. But notice the setting. Jesus looked down and saw the crowds. But instead of going down to them, He went up the mountainside and trained His disciples.

The Sermon on the Mount occupies Matthew 5 through 7, and by the end of it, the crowds had found and encircled Him, and they were amazed at His teaching. So, in chapters 8 and 9, He ministered among them as the disciples watched. Then Matthew 10 opens: "Jesus called his twelve disciples to him and gave them authority." He sent them out with assignments to do the work. This was our Lord's strategy. He was always training others to shoulder the work He began. That's still His method with us.

*I had rather get ten men to work than
to do the work of ten men.*

—D. L. Moody[2]

The only thing Jesus could *not* delegate was His death on the cross. No one else in heaven or earth could die righteously for the sins of the world. But as soon as He had accomplished that task and risen again, what did He do? He commissioned His followers to take His life and love to all the world. The Gospel of Matthew ends with Jesus saying, "All authority in heaven and on earth has been given to Me. Therefore go" (Matthew 28:18–19).

If Jesus couldn't do everything by Himself, neither can we. If Moses couldn't bear the strain of misappropriated work, neither can we. If Peter and the apostles needed to transfer some of their duties to others, so do we.

If you want to be pleasantly productive, you have to ask this question: *What are the things that only I alone can do?* (Or, to put it bluntly), *What am I currently doing that I can persuade, hire out, assign, delegate, or somehow shift to someone else—or release undone?* We can't do everything. We must tackle only what God has given to us. If you're doing anything someone else can do, there's a good chance you're overloading yourself, which leads to burnout and breakdown. In the process, of course, you're withholding from another soul the blessing of doing what God has singularly called him or her to accomplish.

The apostle Paul once couched his advice about a particular issue like this: "If it is possible, as far as it depends on you . . ." (Romans 12:18). My advice in this chapter is: If it is possible, as far as it depends on you, figure out what only you can do; then take everything else and begin finding ways of passing it along to others or retiring it to the regions of the discarded. That's not laziness. That's biblical wisdom, prudent decentralization, and ethical delegation. You need to be free to do what you do best.

Follow your strengths and passions. Build on your assets. Find the way God seems to best use you, and swim with the current. Only do what only you can do. Only you can be a husband or wife to your spouse. Only you can be a parent to your children. Only you can be a grandparent to those youngsters. Only you can fill a unique role in the life of someone who is special to you. Only you can nourish your soul and care for your body in a way that's pleasing to the Lord.

If you have people working under your direction, train and entrust them with the work. We can't just delegate it and dismiss it. We're still responsible for it, but we do it *through* those whom we oversee. As someone said, "It's not what you *expect* but what you *inspect* that gets done." But people who work their way out of a job never fail to find a better one.

Likewise, if you're a parent, share your responsibility with your children in the form of chores. Divide up the household tasks. Researchers at the University of Minnesota studied a group of people from the time they were children until they became young adults. The researchers were particularly interested in what made some of these adults more successful than others. It had little to do with IQ or natural talent. The biggest deciding factor was whether or not these children had grown up in a family that expected their participation in household chores.[3]

Chores teach children to be responsible and to make a contribution to family life. It gives them a sense of self-respect and social responsibility. It invests them with a spirit of teamwork and significance. It imparts a healthy work ethic and teaches them time management skills at an early age.

Sometimes we don't have coworkers or children to whom we can delegate, and we have to pay someone to share our responsibilities. Until my wife became disabled, I took care of the outside of the house and she managed the inside. But when her multiple sclerosis progressed, I had to start doing more of the inside work. I hired a young man to take care of the yard, because I can only do what only I can do.

You can't do everything. Do what you should, delegate what you can, and trust God with the rest.

Fred Smith was a brilliant mentor of leaders. Here's the way he put it: "As I have gotten older, I have found I am more selective, more thorough, more conscious of what I am trying to do. I have learned that activity is not the mark of accomplishment. The more I can delegate tasks that are not uniquely mine, the more attention I can pay to those what are." He continued, "I have run small organizations, and I have run large corporations. I have never been short of time, because I believe I know how to prioritize. I keep for myself the things that only I can do and delegate the rest."[4]

Last night I had supper with Pastor David Jeremiah, and we were talking about our workloads. "Some people talk about priorities," he said, "but I tell people to think in terms of what I call 'posteriorities.' What things are we going to put at the end of the list? In other words, we aren't going to do them. Some years ago I made a list of things I just wasn't going to do anymore." One of those things, he told me, was serving on a particular board. The workload was too heavy, and he realized God hadn't called him to serve there. Someone else could do it just as well or better. If he tried to serve on a lot of boards, he said, he'd be distracted from his true life's work for which God had equipped him.

Likewise, CEO Michael Hyatt has a "Not to Do" list, which he claims is as important (or more so) than his "To Do" list. Writing in his popular blog, Hyatt said that the only way for "super-productive people to continue to grow professionally without going crazy is periodically to decide what they are *not* going to do."[5]

That's how Jesus and the heroes of Scripture managed to accomplish their work. Only do what only you can do. If I were to die tomorrow, the world would go on spinning and nothing much would change. It might create some temporary alterations or sadness for a few people, but by and large everything would continue on as it's been going because no one is indispensable. Remembering that takes a lot of pressure from our shoulders. It's very hard trying to be God. We find soul-rest when we realize He alone is Lord and God, and He has wisely apportioned our tasks and time.

We shouldn't feel guilty when we don't do what isn't assigned. Only do what you can do.

Study Questions for Mastering This Pattern

1. Where are you on the continuum between being vacation-rested and crash-and-burn exhausted?

_____

_____

_____

_____

2. How would you explain Mrs. Charles M. Cowman's statement that rest is not a sedative for the sick but a tonic for the strong?

_____

_____

_____

_____

3. What one thing do you think the Lord would have to do to take better care of yourself?

_____

_____

_____

4. Are you doing anything someone else can do? How can you shift the burden where it belongs?

_____

_____

_____

_____

For more help in applying these principles or for group study or staff training, download my free *Mastering Life Workbook* at RobertJMorgan.com/MasteringLifeWorkbook.

THE SIXTH PATTERN

Operate on Yourself

Why are you cast down, O my soul?
And what are you disquieted within me?
Hope in God; for I shall yet praise Him,
the help of my countenance and my God.

—Psalm 42:11[1]

18

The Art of Strengthening Yourself in the Lord

E van O'Neill Kane was born in Pennsylvania just as the Confederates took Fort Sumter and started the Civil War. His father, Thomas L. Kane, was a major general in the Union Army and was awarded for the bravery he exhibited at the Battle of Gettysburg. His mother, Elizabeth Denniston Wood Kane, was a medical doctor in a day when female physicians were rare. From his father the boy inherited valor, from his mother a love of medicine. Kane grew up during the Gilded Age, when great advancements were being made in industry and science. He went on to become one of the most innovative surgeons of his day, and his life reads like fiction. Some of his experiments became the fodder of medical textbooks for years to come.

In the early 1920s, for example, Dr. Kane was convinced that too many surgical patients were being put to sleep during their operations when localized anesthesia should be used instead. He thought the hazards of general anesthesia were greater than most physicians assumed, and he suggested that many patients would do fine during surgery with a local anesthesia. His opinions encountered skepticism, so Kane set out to prove his point.

During his career, Dr. Kane had performed nearly four thousand appendectomies. In those days, removing one's appendix was considered major surgery requiring a large incision. Kane decided to perform his next appendectomy using only local anesthesia, and he selected his patient carefully. On February 15, 1921, the man was rolled into the operating room. Dr. Kane didn't put the patient to sleep; instead he applied a local anesthesia and went to work slicing through skin and tissues. He found the appendix, removed it, and sewed the man up. The surgery went well, and the patient assured the medical team he had experienced only minor discomfort.

The name of the patient was Dr. Evan O'Neill Kane. The doctor and the patient were the same. Kane had propped himself up on the operating table and, using mirrors to see the affected area, had removed his own appendix. Other doctors were present to observe the procedure and intervene should anything go wrong, but nothing did. Dr. Kane enjoyed a full recovery and the flurry of notoriety that came with it.[2]

As we go through life, we sometimes become infected and inflamed by certain unhealthy attitudes, toxic habits, and infectious sins. We're exposed to a lot of spiritual contamination down here below, and we easily succumb to depression, anger, anxiety, discouragement, bitterness, and all the rest. It's helpful when friends encourage us, and sometimes we need professional counseling. But one of the greatest discoveries we can ever make is learning to operate on ourselves.

David learned this technique after being deprived of the support of his buddy Jonathan. The story of David and Jonathan is the Bible's classic tale of friendship. Jonathan, caught between loyalty for his father and love toward David, tried with all his heart to reconcile the two. He failed, and in the process he put his friend's life in even greater danger. David fled the armies of Israel and, in one low moment, lost his nerve. His faith nearly collapsed. But 1 Samuel 23:16 says, "Saul's son Jonathan went to David at Horesh and helped him find strength in God."

Friends like that are priceless. How often has my wife or a dear friend or mentor helped me find strength in God! I hope I've done that for others. But sometimes such friends aren't able to help us. Sometimes they're not available or they don't know what to do. Perhaps they're too distracted by their own issues. That's what happened to David. A few chapters later, he faced another crisis, one even more terrifying. He was too distraught to function, and this time Jonathan couldn't come to him, being overwhelmed with his own crises. "But," says the Bible, "David strengthened *himself* in the Lord his God" (1 Samuel 30:6; emphasis mine).

The art of strengthening oneself in the Lord is the greatest of all the spiritual disciplines. Sometimes, under the guidance of the Great Physician, we have to open ourselves up, take a look, improve ourselves, talk to ourselves, encourage ourselves, make our own changes, remove an infected attitude or an inflamed habit, and help ourselves become healthier.

This is what the psalmist was doing when he gave himself a pep talk: "Yes, my soul, find rest in God; my hope comes from him. Truly he is my rock and my salvation; he is my fortress, I will not be shaken" (Psalm 62:5–6). And in Psalm 103: "Praise the Lord, my soul; all my inmost being, praise his holy name" (verse 1). In these passages, the writers weren't praying to God. They weren't talking to their readers. They were addressing their own souls. They were operating on and encouraging themselves in the Lord.

All the Bible heroes did this. The forlorn prophet Jeremiah, for example, wrote, "My soul is downcast within me. Yet this I call to mind and therefore I have hope: Because of the Lord's great love we are not consumed, for his compassions never fail. They are new every morning" (Lamentations 3:20–23). He was cast down, but he brought something to his mind. He preached to himself. He reminded himself of God's faithfulness, of mercies new every morning, of divine compassion that never fails. Hope returned to his heart.

The greatest of all the secrets to personal resilience is learning to strengthen ourselves in the Lord. In essence, that means reminding ourselves of God's promises, rekindling a sense of His presence, and preaching to ourselves His stalwart truths in troubled times. Sometimes we are both preacher and congregation, just as Evan O'Neill Kane was both doctor and patient. Sometimes we can't afford to listen to ourselves; we have to preach to ourselves. We have to tell ourselves the truth and remind ourselves of God's Word.

When we begin looking at things as God does, which is the essence of wisdom, hope returns. Patience is renewed. Fellowship is restored. Behavior is corrected. Instead of bleeding over everyone and rehearsing our problems ad nauseam to our friends, we learn to diagnose, treat, and heal ourselves. This is the key to emotional self-sufficiency and spiritual stamina. This technique is vital to being pleasantly productive and to staying healthy of heart.

If it's a sin you're battling, remind yourself of God's commands. If it's self-pity, remind yourself of His cross. If it's embittering anger, remind yourself of His grace. If it's despair, remind yourself of His hope and His heaven. If it's ingratitude, remind yourself of His blessings. If it's anxiety, remind yourself of His providential power. Learn to prepare your own sermons for an audience of one. Preach to yourself, and search the Scriptures for the best texts to use.

In the surgery suite of your local hospital, you'll find scalpels, scissors, calipers, forceps, retractors, hooks, sponges, sutures, and a trayful of sanitized instruments, each engineered with precision. But what instruments are needed for spiritual self-surgery? Our primary tool is a sharp, two-edged scalpel that penetrates even to dividing soul and spirit, and of the joints and marrow. It discerns the thoughts and intents of the heart (see Hebrews 4:12).

Whenever I'm battling infected thoughts or inflamed passions, I have to turn to God's Word. I often say, "Lord, I need a right verse right now. Nothing but the sheer truth of God can overcome my predicament." Whenever we're overwhelmed with something, either in our souls or in our circumstances, we have to shut the door, open the Word, and search the Scriptures until we find a passage that helps us regain perspective. I often know in general terms where to turn—perhaps to the book of Proverbs, perhaps to the epistles of Paul, perhaps to the Psalms. But I have to start reading, looking at each verse carefully, trying to find just the phrase or verse I need.

Several years ago, when facing a group of outspoken critics who wreaked havoc with me, I knew I needed to get away for a couple of days. Katrina and I checked into the Westin Hotel in Chicago, and every morning I went down to the plaza at the John Hancock Tower, bought a cup of coffee from the vendor, and read through 2 Corinthians. During those two or three days, I fell in love with 2 Corinthians. It's the most autobiographical of Paul's letters, and he spoke honestly of the struggles and anxieties of his ministry. I've seldom so identified with a book in the Bible, and I filled my journal with verses that met my needs.

One of the great passages in 2 Corinthians says:

> Therefore we do not lose heart. Though outwardly we are wasting away, yet inwardly we are being renewed day by day. For our light and momentary troubles are achieving for us an eternal glory that far outweighs them all. So we fix our eyes not on what is seen, but on what is unseen, since what is seen is temporary, but what is unseen is eternal. (2 Corinthians 4:16–18)

How those verses revived me! They contain the essence of resilience, the key to operating on ourselves and encouraging ourselves in the Lord—refocusing from the temporary to the eternal, from the situation at hand to the God who has all things in hand. It's a matter of exchanging our perspective for His. This is what it means to encourage yourself in the Lord, and there are many ways to go about it.

On some occasions I've drawn a line down the middle of a page in my notebook. On the left I've listed my emotions and attitudes—this is a particularly helpful technique when deeply troubled—and on the right I've listed Bible verses God has given me to counteract these damaging emotions. Kneeling, I prayed, "Lord, I'm on the left side of the page and You're on the right. Help me step over the line and be where You are."

Now let's take this a step farther. When you take the verses God gives you in these critical moments of life, when you read them so often you know them by heart, when you memorize them without even being aware of having done so—then you've implanted the pure and unadulterated Truth of God into the deepest furrows of your brain. It's like a chip of unassailable hope that starts irradiating its influence in waves, bathing your conscience and subconscious thoughts with its therapeutic influence. The Bible calls this being transformed by the renewing of our minds (Romans 12:2).

As I say in my book about Scripture memory, *100 Bible Verses Everyone Should Know By Heart,* "Bible verses, committed to memory and applied by the Holy Spirit, are the most powerful medications in the whole world. They're a balm for sore hearts, an elixir for low spirits, an immunization for bad habits, a booster shot of high spirits, a pick-me-up for dreary days, and a stimulant for positive nerves."[3]

In strengthening ourselves in the Lord, we want to focus particularly on the promises of God, for the Father has placed a specific promise in Scripture for every problem we'll encounter in life. When we view our circumstances through the lens of God's promises, it colors them with the right hues and we see them in the proper light. The only known way of growing a stronger faith is consistently focusing our attention on God's promises amid our problems and perils.

Samuel Clarke, an 18th-century British nonconformist pastor, wrote of the power and abundance of promises:

> Christians deprive themselves of their most solid comforts by their unbelief and forgetfulness of God's promises. For there is no extremity so great but there are promises suitable to it, and abundantly sufficient for our relief in it. . . . If we would reap the comfort and benefit of these promises, it is not enough that we have them by us, or now and then look into them, but we must thoroughly acquaint ourselves with them, store them up in our memories, and be often meditating upon them, that they may be ready for use when we most want them. . . . At the same time, our eyes must be fixed upon the Lord Jesus Christ, as the only foundation of our hopes, in and through whom alone all the promises are made good to us. . . . Constantly plead the promises with God in prayer. . . . He will acknowledge his own handwriting.[4]

Amen! As we study "His own handwriting," we'll find prescriptions there for every ill. And as we study the Bible carefully and systematically, we'll find it a pharmacy for the soul. Study God's Word in context, and seek out Bible teachers and pastors who are expositors by nature. You'll find that God's Word unfolds in logical layers. When you read the book of Romans, for example, one sentence follows another in rational order, each verse contributing to the unfolding wisdom of each chapter, and each chapter to the whole book. Studying Scripture passages in their context always enhances our understanding of what God's telling us.

Study the predictions and prophecies of the Bible, for the Lord has packed the future into the book He's given us. He's told us what's to come. Study the subject of heaven in Scripture, for God wants to encourage us with our eternal home. Study the prayers of the Bible, for they are patterns for the way God wants us to approach Him. Study the commands of the Bible, for they're the guardrails for life's journey. Study the characters of the Bible, for they comprise the great cloud of witnesses who encourage us to run with perseverance the race before us. Study the benedictions and beatitudes of Scripture, for they encapsulate the blessings God wants to bestow on you today.

Take His Word at face value and rely on its truthfulness. Take God at His word and rely on His faithfulness.

Every morning this week during my daily appointment, I've been reading through the book of Ezra, which is named for one of the Bible's great scholars who is introduced to us in the middle of his book. He went to Jerusalem at a critical time, wanting to reestablish the truth among God's people in Judea. What struck me in my reading this morning was the adjective used to describe him in Ezra 7:6: "This Ezra came up from Babylon. He was a teacher well versed in the Law of Moses, which the Lord, the God of Israel, had given . . . for Ezra had devoted himself to the study and observance of the Law of the Lord, and to teaching its decrees and laws in Israel."

"Well versed"! Pleasantly productive people are well versed; they are versed for life. They know how to strengthen themselves in the Lord through meditation on Scripture, judicious reading, journaling, praying, confession, interruptions from stress, strategic rest, close friendships, a good church, and intentional thanksgiving. They know the secret of cultivating the soul.

"Nourish [your inner self] with good works," wrote William Law in his classic *A Serious Call to a Devout and Holy Life.*

Give it peace in solitude, get it strength in prayer, make it wise with reading, enlighten it by meditation, made it tender with love, sweeten it with humility, humble it with penance, enliven it with Psalms and Hymns, and comfort it with frequent reflections upon future glory. Keep it in the presence of God, and teach it to imitate those guardian angels, through which they attend on human affairs, and the lowest of mankind, yet always behold the face of our Father which is in heaven.[5]

Be emotionally confident and spiritually self-sufficient. Learn to operate on yourself. As you learn the fine art of strengthening yourself in the Lord, the Great Physician Himself infuses you with strength. He will restore your soul. Out of the riches of His grace, He will strengthen you with all power through His Spirit in your inner being; and as your days may demand shall your strength ever be.[6]

That's what God has promised, and that's what we can claim.

Study Questions for Mastering This Pattern

1. Can you describe a time when you operated on yourself? Perhaps you self-corrected a bad habit, steered away from a negative direction, or recovered from a potential mistake.

_____

_____

_____

_____

2. What specific Bible verses have been useful scalpels in operating on yourself at such times?

_____

_____

_____

_____

3. How would you describe to someone else the techniques of encouraging himself or herself in the Lord?

_____

_____

_____

4. In light of this chapter, can you think of a Bible verse to begin memorizing this week?

_____

_____

_____

For more help in applying these principles or for group study or staff training, download my free *Mastering Life Workbook* at RobertJMorgan.com/MasteringLifeWorkbook.

THE SEVENTH PATTERN

Live As If

> *If you want a quality, act as if you already have it.*
>
> —William James[1]

> *Assume a virtue if you have it not.*
>
> —William Shakespeare, *Hamlet*[2]

19

Harness the Psychology of the Soul

When we hear the name *Theodore Roosevelt*, we think of the muscular, mustached man who led his Rough Riders up San Juan Hill, hunted dangerous animals all over the world, and, as president, conducted foreign affairs by speaking softly and carrying a big stick. But as a child, Roosevelt was a weak lad who suffered terrible bouts of asthma, which left him fearful and withdrawn. He described himself as "a rather sickly and awkward boy." He found solace in reading. But his reading changed his life one day when he devoured a seafaring novel by Frederick Marryat, the British Royal Navy officer who began writing fiction during the days of Dickens. Roosevelt recounted in his autobiography:

> When a boy, I read a passage in one of Marryat's books which always impressed me. In the passage the captain of some small British man-of-war is explaining to the hero how to acquire the quality of fearlessness. He says that at the outset almost every man is frightened when he goes into action, but that the course to follow is for the man to keep such a grip on himself that he can act just *as if* he was not frightened. This is the theory upon which I went.[3]

Adopting the philosophy of the fictional British captain, Roosevelt began training himself to act *as if* he were not afraid, *as if* he were not sick, and *as if* he were not sad. He discovered an astonishing psychological fact: our emotions will grudgingly fall into line and follow the attitudes we choose to adopt with our minds. That is, our feelings will gradually follow the choices we *will* for them. "This was the theory upon which I went," Roosevelt said. "There were all kinds of things of which I was afraid at first, ranging from grizzly bears to 'mean' horses and gunfighters; but by acting *as if* I were not afraid I gradually ceased to be afraid. Most men can have the same experience if they choose."[4]

While Theodore Roosevelt was practicing the *as if* principle, another man was writing about it. William James, the father of American psychology, was one of the first to articulate and popularize this concept. James theorized,

> There is no better known or more generally useful precept in the moral training of youth, or in one's personal self-discipline, than that which bids us pay primary attention to what we do and express, and not to care too much for what we feel. . . . By regulating the action, which is under the more direct control of the will, we can indirectly regulate the feeling, which is not. Thus the sovereign voluntary path to cheerfulness, if our spontaneous cheerfulness be lost, is to sit up cheerfully, to look around cheerfully, and to act and speak *as if* cheerfulness were already there. If such conduct doesn't make you soon feel cheerful, nothing else on that occasion can. To feel brave, act *as if* we were brave, use all our will to that end, and a courage fit will very likely replace the fit of fear. Again, in order to feel kindly toward a person to whom we have been inimical, the only way is more or less deliberately to smile, to make sympathetic inquiries, and to force ourselves to say genial things. One hearty laugh together will bring [together] enemies.[5]

This principle works on a psychological level even for nonspiritual folks, for God has built the capacity into every soul for selecting our own attitudes. He's given us the ability to make attitudinal choices. The most powerful expression I've ever read of this is Viktor Frankl's book *Man's Search for Meaning,* with insights forged in the horrors of Auschwitz. When forces beyond our control strip us of everything in life, Frankl said in summary, our last remaining freedom—the one thing that can't be taken from us—is our ability to choose our own attitude in any given set of circumstances.

This general concept has become the basis for a hundred years of motivational speeches, self-help books, and think-and-grow-rich philosophies. The American impresario Lincoln Kirstein founded the New York City Ballet after World War II based on this idea, as gleaned from an odd mystic named George Gurdjieff. "He gave me a method which can be lightly called *as if,*" Kirstein told a magazine. "If you behave *as if* something were true then you make it happen. We thought of a ballet school, a company, Lincoln Center, long before they happened. By behaving *as if* it would happen, we wasted no time."[6]

In addiction recovery programs, this is sometimes called "Fake it till you make it." If you don't feel pleasant, positive, or strong, simply act *as if* you do. Your attitude will catch up with you.

Even when viewed outside the context of Scripture, this technique brings value to life, for it corresponds to the way God made our souls. We live more richly when we live every day *as if* it were our last, or tackle a project *as if* our life depended on it, or go about our work *as if* we were making a difference. At best, this kind of mental exercise can improve our attitudes and enhance our productivity. But at worst, as we've all seen with too-eager salesmen and health-and-wealth preachers, it can also spawn artificiality and hypocrisy.

Though the *as if* principle may be the basis for most of the self-improvement literature of the last century, to be truly effective, it needs a biblical anchor. The *as ifs* need to be squarely based on realities, not platitudes or positivisms. Hebrews 11:27, for example, says about Moses: "By faith he left Egypt, not fearing the anger of the king, for he persevered *as if* he saw the invisible one" (Hebrews 11:27).[7]

Too many people act *as if* there were no God, *as if* God didn't care about their lives or behavior, *as if* God's promises weren't true. But Christians have the unspeakable joy of dealing with *as ifs* that are realities. When viewed from a scriptural context and brought into alignment with God's Word, the *as if* principle is a sure way of talking about faith and obedience. We persevere *as if* seeing Him who is invisible.

Acting *as if* . . . well, that's the essence of faith. From God's perspective, the *as if* isn't imaginary; it's more real than anything else. The simple act of trusting God can be defined as acting *as if* God were going to keep His promises, however bleak the current circumstances may appear. Faith is making an assumption that God will do as He has promised. On the basis of that assumption, we act *as though* the thing were done.

This is one of the hardest and holiest lessons I've ever tried to learn. In my book *The Promise,* I described the power of Romans 8:28, which is the most all-inclusive promise in the Bible: "And we know that in all things God works for the good of those who love him, who have been called according to his purpose."

I wrote in *The Promise*:

What if you knew it would all turn out well, whatever it was you were facing? What if Romans 8:28 really were more than a cliché? What if it was a certainty, a Spirit-certified life preserver, an unsinkable objective truth, infinitely buoyant, able to keep your head above water even when your ship was going down? What if it really worked? What if it always worked? What if there were no problems beyond its reach? Would that make a difference to you?[8]

If we truly believe that promise, we'll learn to act *as if* everything will be all right even when it seems all wrong, for we'll be choosing to live by faith rather than sight. That's an attitude that banishes so much of our worry and discouragement. As Frederick William Faber put it, "Ill that he blesses is our good, and unblessed good is ill; / And all is right that seems most wrong, if it be his sweet will."[9]

David approached Goliath *as if* the giant was as good as defeated. The children of Israel marched around Jericho *as if* certain of victory. Peter got out of the boat *as if* he really could walk on water. The apostles went out evangelizing the world *as if* Christ was alive. All these *as ifs* were based on realities, so it made sense for the biblical heroes to set their sails to heaven's wind and tune their souls to heaven's music.

This is been the secret of the saints of all the ages. Consider what happened to Saint Francis of Assisi. One night he suffered terrible weakness and infirmity of body and spirit. In the midst of his suffering he felt he heard God's voice. "Tell me, brother, if anyone should give thee in return for thy infirmities and sufferings, a treasure so vast and precious that the whole earth by comparison would be as nothing to it, wouldst thou not greatly rejoice?" Francis agreed he would, saying, "Great indeed, O Lord, would be this treasure and very precious."

"Then, brother," replied the voice, "be glad and make merry in thine infirmities and sufferings; and for the rest, thou mayest be assured of My Kingdom, even *as if* thou wert already there."[10] Francis began marching to a divine drummer, basing his attitudes on biblical realities, and living *as if* he were already blessed with every spiritual blessing in the heavenly places.

The opposite, of course, is also true. If you act as if you're depressed, you'll become that way. If you think negatively, you'll become negative and turn others in the same direction. If you act as though all is lost, you'll be swallowed by self-pity. I made this mistake in high school. I'm something of an introvert, but at the time I didn't understand much about personality issues; I only knew I was often lonely. So, to gain the sympathy and attention of my friends, I acted as if I needed moral support. I spoke negatively of myself, expecting them to contradict me and build me up. I got attention by talking about how "worthless" I felt. Of course, the tone of my conversations became a self-fulfilling prophecy. It took years to recover from the battering I gave my self-esteem.

The Bible says, "For as he thinks in his heart, so is he" (Proverbs 23:7).[11] Whether positive or negative, whether in faith or in fear, we will always live *as if*. So we must make sure our *as ifs* are scriptural, true, and pleasantly productive.

The *as if* principle is highly valuable in the way we pray. In an old sermon titled "True Power—True Prayer," Charles Haddon Spurgeon reminds us:

> In prayer, there should always be some definite objects for which we should plead . . . count them as if they were received, reckon them as if you had them already, and act as if you had them—act as if you were sure you should have them. . . . We need a realizing assurance in prayer. To count over the mercies before they are come! To be sure that they are coming! To act as if we had got them! When you have asked for your daily bread, no more to be disturbed with care, but to believe that God has heard you and will give it to you. Count them as if they were received, reckon them as if you already. [12]

Acting *as if* is the essence of faith, and it's also the essence of obedience. Sometimes we have to do what's right, even when we don't feel like it, even when it doesn't appear to make sense. The apostle Paul made this point to the Corinthians, telling them they should commit themselves to God *as if* the world were ending, because seasons of intense persecution loomed ahead.

What I mean, brothers and sisters, is that the time is short. From now on those who have wives should live *as if* they did not; those who mourn *as if* they did not; those who are happy, *as if* they were not; those who buy something, *as if* it were not theirs to keep; those who use the things of the world, *as if* not engrossed in them. For this world in its present form is passing away. (1 Corinthians 7:29–31; italics mine)

Paul told the Ephesians, "Serve wholeheartedly, *as if* you were serving the Lord, not people, because you know that the Lord will reward each one for whatever good they do" (Ephesians 6:7; italics mine). In other words, if you're taking a class in high school or college, imagine Jesus as the professor and pour your heart into the subject in order to learn His truth and make a good grade to please Him. That requires some imagination, but it's an imagination that reflects reality. If you're working on an assembly line, imagine Jesus as the foreman and seek to please Him with your job performance. If you're a homemaker, think of Jesus as the primary resident of the house. Act *as if* you were serving the Lord and it will affect the way you go about your work.

Paul told Timothy to exhort older men *as if* they were his fathers (1 Timothy 5:1). The writer of Hebrews said, "Remember those in prison *as if* you were their fellow prisoners, and those who are mistreated *as if* you yourselves were suffering" (Hebrews 13:3; italics mine).

This calls for sanctified imagination. It means we trust and we obey by faith, making choices of attitude and action based on what God has said in His Word. Years ago I was taught the old train illustration, of the engine, the coal car, and the passenger car. The engine represents the facts, the coal car is our faith, and the caboose is our feelings. They must line up in that order, for if we put our feelings at the head of the line, we'll never make it down the tracks.

Some days I don't feel very happy, but the Bible tells me to rejoice in the Lord anyway. So I must act *as if* I have joy, trusting the true cheerfulness of Jesus to kindle into flame with a few puffs from the billows of the Holy Spirit. Some days I may not feel humble, but I should act with humility—not as a show of pretended modesty, but as sincerely as I can—and true humility will gradually emerge. When we stand in church to sing, it should be *as if* we were standing before the heavenly throne itself.

> *We do not see the things of eternity. We do not see God, or heaven, or the angels, or the redeemed in glory, or the crowns of victory, or the harps of praise; but we have faith in them and this leads us to act as if we saw them. And this is, undoubtedly, the fact in regard to all who live by faith and who are fairly under its influence.*
>
> **—Albert Barnes, in his commentary of Hebrews 11:1**[13]

In the same way, as C. S. Lewis suggested in *Mere Christianity* that even if we don't feel affection for another person, we should act *as if* we did love him or her, for the emotions will follow the behavior.[14]

I'm reminded of the story I heard of the man who wanted to divorce his wife in the most painful possible way. A cunning friend advised him to treat her as if she were a goddess. "For a solid month," advised the friend, "act as though you were passionately in love with her, and then suddenly walk out and leave her devastated." The man implemented the plan, and every day he acted as if he loved his wife with all his heart. At the end of the month he ran into his cunning friend. "How did it go?" asked the friend. "Did you leave your wife?"

"Leave her!" shouted the husband. "How could I leave her? She's a goddess!"[15]

When we act *as if,* the mind-set we select settles into our hearts, we internalize the decision, and the attitudes we've chosen engender the emotions we need.

I can hardly think of a more important technique to teach youngsters. Your children may not want to go to school today, but help them learn to bound up the steps and through the door *as if* they were going to learn something that would change the rest of their lives. They don't want to do their chores, but what if they decided to do them *as though* they were enjoyable? That was Mary Poppins's great lesson, for she knew in every task there was an "element of fun." When we "find the fun—snap!" The job we "undertake becomes a piece of cake."[16]

For nonbelievers, the ability to choose one's attitude may be a great psychological technique. But for Christians, the determination to live a life of faith and obedience brings the *as if* principle to true fruition. We claim the promises of God *as if* they were real—which they are. We obey the commands of God *as if* they were urgent—which they are. We view circumstances *as if* God were on His throne—which He is. We determine to adopt biblical attitudes like love, joy, peace, patience, kindness, and peace, even when we don't feel like it. Somehow in the process we harness the psychology of the soul. Somehow our footsteps begin following the cadence of Christ.

If you act as if you are interested in your job,
that bit of acting will tend to make your inter-
est real. It will also tend to decrease your fa-
tigue, your tensions, and your worries.[17]

—Dale Carnegie

Years ago, I gave my wife, Katrina, a book about enthusiasm. The author claimed that enthusiasm was a kind of faith that had been set afire, and we should plunge into every day with an enthusiastic attitude. We should make ourselves function with enthusiasm even when we don't initially feel it, he said. We should stoke the fires of enthusiasm because it makes the difference in everything we do and with everyone we meet. Sad is the person who outlives the enthusiasm of life, he said. Having enthusiasm is like having two right hands.[18]

A day or so later I came home to find Katrina on the verge of collapse. She looked as though she couldn't make it through supper. I asked the reason. "It's that book about enthusiasm," she said. "I've been living enthusiastically for two days. I've jumped out of bed with enthusiasm, taken the children to school with enthusiasm, run the carts through the grocery aisles with enthusiasm, cleaned the house with enthusiasm, done my chores and my church work with enthusiasm. I've acted as if I were enthusiastic all the time, and I became enthusiastic, and now I'm just enthused out."

Well, we can take anything too far, I suppose, but I'm grateful that we can choose to be enthusiastic, even if our emotions may not agree at the moment. Attitudes are more important than emotions. Emotions come and go, but attitudes come and grow, and our attitudes, when based on scriptural realities, become the seedbed for ever-healthier emotions as we go through the day and throughout the years. The *as if* principle frees us from being enslaved to our emotions or to our circumstances. We can choose to act other than we feel, and over prolonged periods, we can work our way up from depression, from discouragement, from loneliness, from lethargy and boredom. We can live enthusiastically.

This has meant so much to me. Born a melancholic and given to depression, I'm not sure what would have happened to me if I hadn't realized I can take charge of my own attitudes and put them under the Spirit's control. Rather than hearing the soulful tunes of my own negative feelings, I can turn the dial, change the station, choose a biblical frequency, and select a set of attitudes that harmonizes with heaven.

Sainted mystic Brother Lawrence, said long ago about practicing the presence of God:

> The time of business does not with me differ from the time of prayer, and in the noise and clatter of my kitchen, while several persons are at the same time calling for different things, I possess God in as great tranquility *as if* I were upon my knees at the Blessed Sacrament. . . . I began to live *as if* there was none but He and I in the world.[19]

Learn to cultivate positive attitudes that reflect divine realities. Learn to live as if God's Word was true—for it is. Decide to be positive in spirit on the basis of God's promises. Choose to rejoice on the basis of His Word. Remember Abraham Lincoln's comment that people are about as happy as they make up their minds to be. Shake off the melancholy melodies of life and put on the headphones of heaven. You'll be like someone locking into a new wavelength, hearing a new song and picking up a new beat in life, and marching through Immanuel's ground to fairer worlds on high. As Henry David Thoreau wrote, "If a man does not keep pace with his companions, perhaps it is because he hears a different drummer. Let him step to the music which he hears, however measured or far away."[20]

Study Questions for Mastering This Pattern

1. The "as if" principle could turn us into hypocritical actors or it could lead us to a life of faith. What's the subtle difference between those two applications of this teaching?

_____

_____

_____

_____

2. As you read this material, did any area of your life come to mind? How and where could you apply this teaching?

_____

_____

_____

_____

3. How can the "as if" principle help improve your personality?

_____

_____

_____

_____

For more help in applying these principles or for group study or staff training, download my free _Mastering Life Workbook_ at RobertJMorgan.com/MasteringLifeWorkbook.

THE EIGHTH PATTERN

Bathe in the Dead Sea

When Handel was asked why his mu-
sic was so cheerful, he replied,
"I can't make any other. I write as I feel.
When I think on God my heart is so full of joy
that the notes dance and leap from my pen."

—George Frideric Handel[1]

20

The Singular Secret of
Unsinkable Saints

Come with me to the arid shorelines of the world's most desolate lake. No one ever fishes there, for fish can't survive its toxic waters. There's no swimming or waterskiing, for it's risky to be splashed in the eyes. The heat is often blistering, and, as an added note, it's in the middle of an area rent with political strife. Yet the Dead Sea is one of the most popular therapeutic destinations on earth. Its beaches are filled with bathers caking themselves with mud, its minerals are packaged and sold all over the world, and bathers boast of the restorative nature of its waters.

The Dead Sea occupies the lowest elevation in the world, at 1,400 feet below sea level. The currents of the Jordan River flow into it, but no water flows out. It has no outlet except evaporation. As the waters are drawn up by the withering heat of the Negev Desert, a heavy saline and mineral content remains, which has accrued for millennia. As a result, the Dead Sea, a place of bleak and barren beauty, is nearly ten times as salty as the ocean and much denser than the human body. That's why bathers bob on its surface like a cork.

I've taken several refreshing dips in the Dead Sea over the years, and it's great fun to float around like driftwood, buoyed by the water in a way that totally relaxes every muscle. You can lean back in the Dead Sea and read a newspaper as if sitting in a folding chair.

To me, floating in the Dead Sea is a picture of the unsinkable density of the waters of joy described in Scripture. The body of Bible verses about joy represents a virtual ocean of encouragement—a living one, to be sure, but just as buoyant to the soul as the Dead Sea is to the body. The joy of the Lord pushes us upward, keeps us afloat on choppy waters, refreshes us in desert places, and helps us resurface when pulled down by the undertows of life.

We sometimes face circumstances that overwhelm us. The prophet Jeremiah, melancholic to the core, once cried in distress: "The waters closed over my head, and I thought I was about to perish" (Lamentations 3:54). But he knew the secret of unsinkability, as he told us elsewhere: "Your words were found, and I ate them, and Your word was to me the *joy* and *rejoicing* of my heart" (Jeremiah 15:16; emphasis mine).[2] Cheerful Christians have an unsinkable quality because we're supported by the joy of the Lord and by the salient waters of His Word.

One summer when I was a boy, our church had a picnic at a swimming pool near Watauga Lake in East Tennessee. There my Sunday school teacher, Rome Bailey, taught me how to float on my back. I was jittery during the lesson; I couldn't swim very well. But Mr. Bailey gently supported me with his hands and told me to calm down and rest my head back on the water. "Let the pool work for you," he said. "If you'll relax, the water will hold you up."

Since this was a freshwater pool and not the Dead Sea, I found it hard to do; but it was a preview of a harder lesson I've tried to learn since. To stay emotionally buoyant on the lake of life, we have to learn to float in the waters of God's joy, supported by His everlasting arms. In doing so, we find we're unsinkable, not because of the makeup of our constitution but because of the composition of His joy.

This is harder for some of us to learn than for others. God has created our personalities as uniquely as He did our bodies. Some people are melancholic in temperament; others are sanguine in nature. Many people have been relatively unscathed by troubles, whereas others have faced traumatic circumstances that have left them wounded, worried, and chronically discouraged.

Yet our personalities are not set in cement, and our circumstances cannot determine the caliber of the soul. Previously in *Mastering Life Before It's Too Late,* we've talked about the techniques of operating on ourselves, encouraging ourselves in the Lord, choosing our own attitudes, and learning to live *as if.* Here's the next step. Because of who God is and what Jesus has done, we can determine to be cheerful people; we can choose an attitude of gladness; we can bathe in His joy and discover the secret of unsinkability.

My friend Tom Tipton, one of America's great African American gospel singers, learned the secret of unsinkability at a young age. He told me of being a shoeshine boy in Washington, D.C., in the early 1940s, when a shine went for a dime. Once when he was eight years old, as he was working outside the White House, he heard about an exciting event for the following Monday—the White House Easter Egg Roll. He decided to go, but when he showed up at the gate with the other children, the guard wouldn't let him in. He was told he didn't belong there. He was a little black boy.

In distress, Tom ran home to his mother and told her what happened. "Junior, don't worry," she said. "Just love everybody." Not satisfied with that, he ran to his father, who told him, "Junior, don't worry about that. Just be the best shoeshine boy you can be." That advice of his parents, Tom told me, established his attitudes for life. Even as a child he realized he could take charge of his reactions, love others, be joyful, and do his best at whatever God assigned him.

That's not the whole story. On Tuesday after the Easter Egg Roll, Tom returned to his shoeshine spot, and from outside the iron fence, he said loudly, "One of these days I'll be back, and I will go inside that big White House and they will call me Mr. Tipton."

And that's what happened. The days came when he sang for

presidents and rubbed shoulders with world leaders, who called him Mr. Tipton. When he later wrote it all down in his autobiography, he gave it the title *Shining Out and Shining In*.[3]

He was unsinkable! Imagine the effect of thoroughly studying for yourself the subject of unsinkability in Scripture! Some years ago I decided to investigate every reference to *joy* in the Bible. I selected a handful of joyful terms—*joy, cheer,* and *gladness*—and I sought out every occurrence of these words from Genesis to Revelation. It's a study I've never finished. There are too many references to process. Using only these three or four key terms, I developed a list of 751 references in 477 verses, and further cross-references on those verses led to other passages expressing similar sentiments. Add the words *happiness, blessed,* and *hopeful* to the mix, and the verses charge at you like stampeding buffalo. I was overcome by the sheer preponderance of this topic and its intertwining threads in Scripture.

Though it's an unconcluded study, I've come away with some principles I'd like to share in this chapter. They've been personality-altering for me. No exercise under heaven can be more uplifting to our perspectives and salutary to our personalities. As we dip our toes into this subject, here are some things we learn.

First, God's very personality is full of joy. He is a God of joy. He is joyful in His essence, to the unfathomable core of His being. His character radiates joy like the sun radiating light, and it's impossible for us to experience genuine joy without conceptualizing the joyfulness of the Divine. When the Bible talks about the joy of the Lord, it's not just referring to the joy God *gives* but the joy He *possesses* within Himself. Psalm 104:31 says God rejoices in all He has made. Jesus was anointed by the Father with the "oil of gladness" (Hebrews 1:9)[4] and the joy He bestowed on His disciples was nothing less than the distribution of His own infinite joy into their hearts. He was described as "full of joy through the Holy Spirit" (Luke 10:21), and He promised His disciples would experience "the full measure of my joy within them" (John 17:13). The perception that God is akin to a grumpy old man is a satanic lie that casts a depressing shadow over our spirits. The Bible says He rejoices over us with singing (Zephaniah 3:17).

Second, God's home is a joyful place. Heaven is everlastingly happy. In His presence is fullness of joy (Psalm 16:11). "Strength and joy are in His dwelling place," says 1 Chronicles 16:27. What an environment! If our present world brims with joy, sinful though it is, imagine the atmosphere of heaven. The radiance of the joy of the Lord floods every square foot of the real estate of the Celestial City. That's why His faithful followers will someday hear Him say, "Well done, good and faithful servant. . . . Enter into the joy of your Lord" (Matthew 25:23).[5]

Third, we should pay attention to the joy God has woven into all His creation. According to Job 38:7, the angels sang together and shouted for joy as God created the world. Psalm 19:5 pictures the sun as rising each day like a champion rejoicing to run his course through the sky. First Chronicles 16:33 says, "Let the trees of the forest sing, let them sing for joy before the Lord." The psalmist enjoined the universe to reflect the joy of the Creator:

> Shout for joy to the Lord, all the earth. . . .
> Let the sea resound and everything in it,
> the world, and all who live in it.
> Let the rivers clap their hands,
> let the mountains sing together for joy. (Psalm 98:4, 7–8)

Joy is the natural state of the creation, for its Maker is the God who dwells in uninterrupted and infinite joy. Even though the world is presently under the curse of sin, the whole creation yet vibrates with joy. Just listen to the birds singing by day, the concert of the crickets and frogs by night, the gurgling of forest brooks and the roar of mighty waterfalls, the rhythmic crashing of the sea against the coastline. According to the book of Job, the wings of the ostrich flap joyfully and the horse rejoices in his strength (Job 38:11, 39:21). According to Psalm 89:12, mountains like Mount Tabor and Mount Hermon sing for joy at the name of the Lord. Psalm 96:12–13 shouts: "Let the fields be jubilant and everything in them; let all the trees of the forest sing for joy. Let all creation rejoice before the Lord." God has tuned His entire cosmos to the strains of gladness.

Yet it's a tarnished joy, for when sin broke out on earth it sent a chill through the universe. Death, mourning, and despair fell like a shroud over the human race. That's why Christ came—to give the "oil of joy instead of mourning, and a garment of praise instead of a spirit of despair" (Isaiah 61:3). Our Lord's birth announcement, made by angelic heralds to the shepherds over the fields of Bethlehem, said, "Behold, I bring you good tidings of great joy which will be to all people" (Luke 2:10).[6]

That's our fourth truth: Jesus came to reinstate joy to His creation. Notice how the book of Acts—the story of new Christians spreading the gospel despite opposition—is filled with references to joy. In his sermon on the Day of Pentecost, Peter referred to Jesus as a man filled with joy (Acts 2:28). Those who received His message were seized with joy. "Every day they devoted themselves to meeting together in the temple complex, and broke bread from house to house. They ate their food with a joyful and humble attitude" (Acts 2:46).

Even when the apostles were flogged for continuing their public ministry, they "left the Sanhedrin, rejoicing" (Acts 5:41). When Philip took the gospel to a city in Samaria, "there was great joy in that city" (Acts 8:8). When the Ethiopian was baptized, "he went on his way rejoicing" (Acts 8:39). When Barnabas saw the growth of the gospel in the city of Antioch, he was glad and filled with joy (Acts 11:23). The disciples in Acts 13:52 "were filled with joy and with the Holy Spirit." Paul told his listeners in the town of Lystra: "He fills your hearts with joy" (Acts 14:17). When Paul and Silas were beaten and imprisoned in Philippi, they sang hymns at midnight, and the jailer was converted: "He was filled with joy because he had come to believe in God—he and his whole household" (Acts 16:34). Wherever the gospel spread in the book of Acts, joy followed. Their joy was unspeakable and full of glory (1 Peter 1:8).

Fifth, Christians therefore have a sacred obligation to live joyfully. Joy is the duty of the Christian. According to Ecclesiastes 5:20, we should be "occupied with joy."[7] Psalm 33:1 says, "Sing joyfully to the Lord, you righteous; it is fitting for the upright to praise him." Psalm 65:8 adds, "Where morning dawns, where evening fades, you call forth songs of praise." God intends His people to display enduring joy from sunup to sundown. He also gives us songs in the night. We're to rejoice in the Lord always (Philippians 4:4). Jonathan Edwards, the colonial-era theologian of Massachusetts, said God has called His people to be "distinguishingly happy."[8]

We perform a great disservice to the Lord when we mope around as if all is lost. A gloomy Christian is a poor illustration of the faith. This doesn't mean we are always ecstatic and gleeful. The heroes of the Bible displayed a full range of emotions, and Jesus wept by the tomb of His friend Lazarus. None of us knows what may befall us day by day, and the joy of the Lord doesn't rescind all heartache.

Just today I had lunch with a friend of mine, Lloyd Byers, whose son—Captain Josh Byers, a West Point graduate and military hero—died in Iraq when his vehicle hit a roadside bomb. Josh's Humvee had been first in a convoy moving to set up a new camp in Fallujah. He was in the front passenger seat, and Sergeant Tim Buskell was driving. When the explosion occurred, Sergeant Buskell was blown out of the Humvee, but he was holding onto the steering wheel so tightly he pulled himself back in. "My body went out and came back in almost simultaneously," he said. His instinct told him to slam on the brakes, but through the smoke and confusion he heard Captain Byers say in a gravelly voice, "Sergeant, we've hit an IED. Keep moving forward."[9]

Buskell hit the gas and moved forward a few yards, which, as it turned out, saved at least two other lives. When he brought the disabled Humvee to a stop, he looked over and saw his captain as if in a peaceful sleep. The medic declared Josh dead.

Captain Josh Byers was a committed Christian with an outspoken testimony among his soldiers, and his last words, "Keep moving forward," became the motto for all who knew him. Those three words sustained his parents and siblings, and they also became the title of a book telling the story of Josh Byers's life: *Keep Moving Forward: My Son's Last Words*, by Dr. Lloyd Byers.

Lloyd told me, "When the numbness began to wear off after the devastating news of Josh, I lost my joy. In fact, I got angry with God for a while and afterward I dealt with much guilt since I had served as a minister of the gospel and a foreign missionary teaching others about the joy of the Lord. God just loved me through my hurt and struggle and I quickly realized how powerful, patient, and kind His love is.

"It was not until a friend shared with me Isaiah 57:1 that I learned I could have joy in my life again. 'The righteous perish, and no one takes it to heart; the devout are taken away, and no one understands that the righteous are taken away to be spared from evil.' I read that with a heavy heart, but God shouted to me in my pain.

"I now can continually praise the Lord as the joy of the Lord is my strength," Lloyd said. "One day I'll be in heaven with Jesus and my son forever, but for now I can rejoice that Josh doesn't have to deal with this world of heartache and pain. I can continually keep moving forward filled with joy."[10]

The joy of the Lord is the only dynamic that enables us to

keep moving forward at life's hardest moments. This kind of joy doesn't cancel the difficult moments of life, but it does transcend life's circumstances. The apostle Paul summed it up in a couple of phrases in 2 Corinthians: "Sorrowful, yet always rejoicing. . . . In all our troubles my joy knows no bounds" (2 Corinthians 6:10, 7:4). It is possible to be sorrowful yet rejoicing, and to have boundless joy despite troubles. That's the unsinkable pattern of pleasantly productive people.

A Prayer for Joy
Be alone and evermore my hope, my whole trust, my
riches, my delight, my gladness and my joy, my rest and my
calm repose, my peace and my sweet content, my fragrance
and my sweetness, my food and my refreshment, my refuge
and my help, my wisdom, my portion, my own possession
and my treasure, in whom my mind and my heart are fixed
and rooted firmly and immovably for evermore. Amen.

—Saint Bonaventura[11]

Sixth, we should become specialists in joyology, in the theology of joy, or, as Christians of earlier eras called it, "cheerful piety."[12] We must guard our minds against chronic despondency like a Roman sentry protecting his hometown.

Remember what I earlier said about the difference between emotions and attitudes? Emotions come and go; attitudes come and grow. When there's a growing infrastructure of spiritual joy in our minds, we'll better know how to deal with our ups and downs. As we grow in spiritual maturity, there's an inexorable progress that takes us from enjoying the pleasures of the moment to experiencing the joy of the Lord. Our joy has the capacity of increasing, for joy can be cultivated. It can mature. We can have a stronger, larger, richer joy as the years pass. Our personalities can improve.

Devotional writer Hannah Whitall Smith wrote in *The Unselfishness of God and How I Discovered It*:

> Everything that is only a matter of feeling, and not of conviction, is at the mercy of a thousand untoward influences. I learned in time therefore not to seek emotions, but to seek only for convictions, and I found to my surprise and delight that my convictions brought me a far more stable and permanent joy than many of my more emotional friends seemed to experience. . . . All this took me many years in learning. But meanwhile the joy and power of the glorious secret we had discovered grew every year more and more practical; and more and more my soul learned to rest in absolute confidence on the keeping and saving power of the Lord.[13]

Perhaps the Bible's greatest passage on this is found at the end of the obscure Old Testament book of Habakkuk. After listening to the voice of the Lord amid great distress, the prophet cycled to this conclusion at the end of his book:

> *Though the fig tree does not bud*
> *and there are no grapes on the vines,*
> *though the olive crop fails*
> *and the fields produce no food,*
> *though there are no sheep in the pen*
> *and no cattle in the stalls,*
> *yet I will rejoice in the Lord,*

I will be joyful in God my Savior.
The Sovereign Lord is my strength;
he makes my feet like the feet of a deer,
he enables me to tread on the heights. (Habakkuk 3:17–19)

It took Habakkuk the length of an entire book of the Bible to reason his way through his confusion until he reached that outcome. Even the giants of Scripture and the greatest of saints have to process the distresses of life and work on maturing their joy in the Lord.

When I visit the Dead Sea, I never jump into it as I would into a Tennessee lake or a freshwater pool. The minerals are too intense and I don't want to get them in my eyes or mouth. I walk into the water tentatively, go deeper step by step, and finally bend my knees, lean back, and feel the energy of the lake pushing my legs toward the surface like an air bubble. Suddenly I'm floating.

The joy of the Lord is concentrated, intense, and powerful; and as we continue in our Christian walk, bend our knees in prayer, and feel God's presence around us, we come to a place of relaxation and letting the joy of the Lord carry us. It's not a matter of trying to work up happiness, but of letting Him bear our weight and lift us upward.

"Do not grieve, for the joy of the LORD is your strength" (Nehemiah 8:10). That wonderful little verse—I'll say more about it later—is recorded in the book of Nehemiah, the Bible's classic book on the subject of leadership. The chapters of Nehemiah were written against the backdrop of the return of the Babylonian exiles. Years before, in 587 BC, the survivors of Judah were deported to refugee camps hundreds of miles from home. Their great capital of Jerusalem was in ruins, their nation erased from history, their homes gone, their temple destroyed. In Babylon, they sat down and wept and hung their harps on the willow trees and refused to sing (Psalm 137:1–4).

But, according to Nehemiah, years later, when they were allowed to return to Judah, these exiles took their harps with them and began singing again. Many of the returning exiles were professional musicians—singers in the choirs, instrumentalists, composers, arrangers, performers. They were ready to restore joy and praise and worship to Israel. As they went home, they had to decide where to live. Evidently they wanted the opportunity to collaborate whenever they wished. So, Nehemiah 12:29 explains, "The musicians had built villages for themselves around Jerusalem."

What an interesting picture: musical towns and singing villages. Imagine living in a singing village, waking up to song, going to bed to song, hearing the music wafting out of practice halls and upstairs bedrooms, hearing people practicing the harp and lyre. Hearing songs old and new, day and night.

I'm not a musician, but I think I would have enjoyed living in one of those towns. In fact, that's the address of all Spirit-filled Christians. We all live in that zip code. God's very personality is full of joy, and joy is His environment. His universe was spun with the threads of joy, and because of Christ we have an obligation to live joyfully; it's our happy duty.

In the next few pages, I'll show you how essential this is to maintaining our influence, as well as a basic technique for cultivating this attitude. But for now, I'll simply say it helps when we visualize ourselves living in the village of Praise and bathing daily in the sea of God's joy. Though we're not all musically gifted, every heart can be tuned to the music of heaven and to the joy of the Lord. This is what keeps our souls above the circumstances and our heads above the water. It's what keeps us moving forward.

It's the singular secret of unsinkable saints.

When I met Christ,
I felt that I had swallowed sunshine.

—Missionary E. Stanley Jones[1]

Cheerfulness keeps up a kind of daylight in the mind,
and fills it with a steady and perpetual serenity.

—Joseph Addison[2]

21

The Executive Joy of Pleasantly Productive Leadership

I was coming home from a working trip to Europe on April 7, 2006, exhausted and dreading the flight because I was returning to a prickly set of problems. A handful of difficult people were causing trouble, and it was starting to paralyze me. Settling into a window seat, I opened my journal and listed five challenges I knew I'd face the moment I stepped off the plane. I described them as "thorns," though that was charitable. After jotting these woe-is-me items in my notebook, I slid it aside and opened my Bible. I started reading where I had left off the day before, which was in Paul's letter to the Colossians. My eyes fell on the phrase *giving joyful thanks to the Father*, in Colossians 1:12.

We're not just to give thanks, but *joyful* thanks.

That text led to another, and to another, and soon I had jotted down fifteen Bible verses on the subject of joy, writing them in my journal right under my list of "thorns." I instantly knew God wanted me to return home with an attitude of joyful thanksgiving. With effort, I decided then and there to employ executive joy, by God's grace to jump back into my routine and lead others with gladness, whatever the circumstances. It's as if the Lord said to me, "If you return home defeated and down in the dumps, you'll lose your influence and things will go from bad to worse. But if you lead with joy, your people will follow you anywhere."

When the plane landed on that spring day in 2006, I planted a smile on my face, acted *as if* I really felt all the joy I needed to exhibit, took a day or so to recover from jet lag, and plunged into my work with those fifteen verses in my heart. The next months were so difficult I could not have weathered them without the high-flying joy of the Lord, which was available according to the Scriptures He had provided on that flight.

That's what led to my subsequent study of the words *joy, cheer, glad,* and *happy,* which occur 751 times in 477 different verses. In the next segment I'll share some of the verses the Lord gave me and how we can use them to fortify our spirits, but three of my favorite Bible verses about cheer and gladness are found in one chapter— Proverbs 15. They provide a trio of truths for high altitude cheer: the capacity to lead others with gladness and confidence.

The first verse is Proverbs 15:13: "A happy heart makes the face cheerful, but heartache crushes the spirit." Our faces are reflectors of the soul. Leaders need an easy smile and a countenance of wisdom and winsomeness. Psalm 34:5 says, "Those who look to him are radiant." When Aaron and all the Israelites saw Moses, his face was radiant (Exodus 34:30). Ecclesiastes 8:1 says, "A person's wisdom brightens their face and changes its hard appearance." The Old Testament phrase "rejoice in the Lord" used the verb *samah,* which has its root in the Hebrew term meaning "to shine, to be bright."[3] The phrase could be rendered, "Brighten up in the Lord." Robert Louis Stevenson said that when a happy person comes into a room, "it is as if another candle has been lighted."[4]

Leaders need wise and happy hearts so their faces will convey vision and enthusiasm. Whether we're leading a family, a softball team, a church, a small business, or a billion-dollar enterprise, we've got to inspire confidence and cheer in those we're serving. The inner cultivation of joy is arguably the greatest tool of effective leaders, because their attitudes will inexorably disseminate like a rolling fog into the hearts of those who follow them.

Leaders create their own climates. It was this atmospheric joy that impressed the queen of Sheba when she visited King Solomon. She told him,

> The report I heard in my own country about your achievements and your wisdom is true. But I did not believe these things until I came and saw with my own eyes. . . . How happy your people must be! How happy your officials, who continually stand before you and hear your wisdom! Praise be to the Lord your God, who has delighted in you and placed you on the throne of Israel. (1 Kings 10:6–9)

Solomon, who was the author of our verses about cheerfulness in Proverbs 15, practiced what he preached, and his optimistic spirit spread throughout his kingdom and beyond.

How, then, can we keep our hearts happy and our faces cheerful? The answer is in the second verse, Proverbs 15:15: "The cheerful heart has a continual feast." There's a simple equation that's been immortalized in leadership literature, poems, proverbs, hymns, and folk songs for centuries. We all have positives and negatives in life, just like electrical currents. We can't ignore either, and both add depth to our days. But our attitudes are determined by where we focus our thoughts. Do we accentuate the positive or underscore the negative? Without a vital relationship with Jesus Christ, our most sensible course is to emphasize the negative. But for Jesus followers, the most rational thing in the world is to accentuate the positive.

God has already guaranteed all things to work for the good to those who love Him, and into the conformity of the purposes of His will (Romans 8:28; Ephesians 1:11). He has given us all things richly to enjoy (1 Timothy 6:17). We haven't been given the spirit of fear, but of power, love, and sound thinking (2 Timothy 1:7). Every needed resource is available through the Holy Spirit who flows from our inmost beings like rivers of living water (John 7:38). From the fullness of His grace, we have all received one blessing after another (John 1:16).[5] He has forbidden discouragement on the basis of His continual presence; He will never leave us or forsake us (Joshua 1:9). Jesus came to give us life more abundantly (John 10:10). Our cups overflow, and goodness and mercy follow us all the days of our lives (Psalm 23:5–6). Our labor is never in vain (1 Corinthians 15:58), and His grace is sufficient in all exigencies (2 Corinthians 12:9). "To live is Christ and to die is gain" (Philippians 1:21), and heaven is only a heartbeat away for God's children. Cheerful people find joy in little things, splendor in the ordinary, elegance in the everyday, and gladness in the greatness and smallness of creation. As the hymnist said, we have "strength for today and bright hope for tomorrow / blessings all mine, with ten thousand beside!"[6]

The Five "Be of Good Cheer" Statements of Jesus

- *Be of good cheer; your sins are forgiven you.* (Matthew 9:2)[7]

- *Be of good cheer, daughter; your faith has made you well.* (Matthew 9:22)[8]

- *Be of good cheer! It is I; do not be afraid.* (Matthew 14:27)[9]

- *Be of good cheer, I have overcome the world.* (John 16:33)[10]

- *Be of good cheer . . . you must also bear witness.* (Acts 23:11)[11]

We should train ourselves to count our blessings, minimize our complaints, rejoice in the Lord, and obey the words of Jesus, "Be of good cheer." The apostle Paul told us to focus our thoughts on what is true, noble, right, pure, lovely, admirable, excellent, and praiseworthy (Philippians 4:8).

Ernest Hemingway once wrote, "If you're lucky enough to have lived in Paris as a young man, then wherever you go for the rest of your life, it stays with you, for Paris is a moveable feast."[12] I love Paris—it's the City of Lights. But I'd rather have the promise in Proverbs from the Father of heavenly lights, for those who truly know Him have a continual feast and enjoy the lasting wonder of intractable cheer.

The third verse in the trio, Proverbs 15:30, goes a step further, telling us about the effect this attitude will have on others. "Light in a messenger's eyes brings joy to the heart, and good news gives health to the bones." In other words, when we approach or provide leadership for others with happy expressions on our faces, with natural smiles and a twinkle in our eyes, the joy leaps from us into their own hearts. When we feel optimistic, it strengthens the morale of those watching us. When we speak positive words, it makes others feel healthier. Bright eyes and a cheerful expression boost the morale of those within our zone of influence.

Joy and gloom are both contagious. Our attitudes are transferable. As a husband and father, if I am angry, anxious, depressed, or withdrawn, it'll impact everyone who lives under my roof. I'll pull down everyone's spirit like a sinker on a fishing line. The same is true in my role as a pastor, as I realized just in time in 2006. But it is possible by grace to be *upbeat* instead of *beat up*. If we practice the Mastering Life techniques and encourage ourselves in the Lord, we'll be fit for leadership, whatever comes.

Dwight D. Eisenhower was keenly aware of the role of executive joy in the days leading up to the Allied Invasion of North Africa in November of 1942. He wrote,

Optimism and pessimism are infectious and they spread more rapidly from the head downward than in any other direction. Optimism has a most extraordinary effect upon all with whom the commander comes in contact. With this clear realization, I firmly determined that my mannerisms and speech in public would always reflect the cheerful certainty of victory—that any pessimism and discouragement I might ever feel would be reserved for my pillow.[13]

In military terms, this is esprit de corps—a shared spirit of enthusiasm among the troops reflecting the confidence of their commanders—and it's a vital practice for leaders everywhere. The most successful coaches are the ones whose enthusiasm is infectious. Among politicians, those who win elections are almost invariably the ones who project transmittable optimism. That's why Roosevelt ("Happy Days Are Here Again") beat Hoover in 1932; why Eisenhower ("I Like Ike!") beat Stevenson in 1952 and 1956; why Kennedy ("A Time for Greatness") defeated Nixon in 1960; why Reagan ("It's Morning in America") won two terms in office; and why Barack Obama ("Hope and Change") defeated the plain-talking John McCain in 2008.

This was the very point of failure for the Children of Israel in the book of Numbers. When ten of their spies reconnoitered the land and returned with defeated attitudes, their gloom spread through the camp like smallpox. Not even the galvanized faith of Joshua and Caleb could counteract the viral effects of these ten dispirited spies. As a result, the nation wandered around as in a daze for forty years till everyone was dead—except Joshua and Caleb, who were finally able to inspire the younger generation to take up the challenge and give birth to the land of Israel.

The story of King David provides a similar lesson. When his son Absalom revolted and drove him from Jerusalem, David's loyal troops defended their king and recaptured the throne. Instead of celebrating the victory, David, understandably, was distraught about the tragedy that had befallen his family and the death of his rebellious son. Retreating to a private room over the gateway, he wept and wailed, crying, "O my son Absalom! My son, my son Absalom! If only I had died instead of you—O Absalom, my son, my son!" (2 Samuel 18:33). According to the next chapter: "For the whole army the victory that day was turned into mourning because on that day the troops heard it said, 'The king is grieving for his son.' The men stole into the city that day as men steal in who are ashamed when they flee from battle" (2 Samuel 19:2).

General Joab, alarmed at how the king's depression was demoralizing the army, marched into David's room and told him plainly,

> Today you have humiliated all your men, who have just saved your life and the lives of your sons and daughters. . . . You have made it clear today that the commanders and their men mean nothing to you. . . . Now go out and encourage your men. I swear by the LORD that if you don't go out, not a man will be left with you by nightfall. This will be worse for you than all the calamities that have come on you from your youth till now. (2 Samuel 19:5–7)

Jolted from languor, the king got up, washed his face, changed his attitude, adjusted his countenance, corrected his posture, took his seat in the gateway, and sent an attitudinal about-face to his troops. Whether he felt like it or not, it was imperative he transmit assurance to his men. Aided by God and through a sheer choice of attitude, David radiated joyful thanksgiving. His courage inspired the army as quickly as his depression had demoralized them.

This is the Spirit-disciplined attitude. It's not just a matter of stoicism or fatalism; nor does it involve being bubbly and fizzy and carbonated. It's not a matter of having an effervescent personality or being a hail-fellow-well-met. It's the reflection of a stewarded sense of thankful joy that runs deeply and quietly through the hearts of God's best leaders. It's Spirit-driven determination. It's God-given courage. It's cruising at the altitude of biblical attitudes, not just for ourselves but for the sake of those we influence.

Be seriously cheerful, and cheerfully serious. Religion was never design'd to make our pleasures less.

—Isaac Watts[14]

Think of a row of standing dominoes. With one push of the finger we can all make dominoes topple over, but Christian leaders can also create a chain reaction that resets all the dominoes in their upright positions, one after another, almost as if by magic. Here's a pedestrian example: if you're surly and unpleasant at the coffee bar tomorrow morning, you may cause the employees behind the counter to start the day with anger and aggravation. They'll pass that along to others, and your attitude will have a domino effect that lasts all day and infects many people. But if you're pleasant and cheerful, if you say a good word and offer a compliment, if you're patient even when displeased with the service and try to lift the spirits of those around you—well, the pass-along effect will ripple through the day and may well affect how a husband greets his wife that night on the other side of the country, or a mom her children. Just as a negative word spreads from person to person in a ripple effect lasting all day, a smile will do the same. That's true for all of us. But when leaders are the ones creating the domino effect, the impact is amplified, for they influence larger numbers of people.

Early in my career, in the mid-1980s, I suffered a spell of discouragement. This was during a time when the literature of leadership was suggesting transparency. Effective leaders, we were told, should be as translucent as glass so our followers could learn authenticity. One night in low spirits I had a meeting with my leadership team. They came into the room laughing and joking and talking about sports and players and wins. When the meeting began, I started talking and opened my soul to them, told them I was discouraged, told them all the reasons why things weren't going well. I can still remember how their faces grew longer until, by the time we dismissed, we were so low we could have sneaked under the crack at the bottom of the door. Driving home, I realized I had just demoralized my whole leadership team, a mistake I resolved never to repeat.

This doesn't mean, of course, that we should never discuss problems or display grief. The heroes and leaders of the Bible often expressed their sorrows, and they were honest about their circumstances. But they did so with the knowledge that the Lord was in His holy temple and on His heavenly throne, and things are never as bad as they seem where the Lord is concerned. In 1 Kings 19, Elijah thought he was the only godly man remaining in Israel; but the Lord knew of seven thousand others (1 Kings 19:18). Elijah, in his defeated mood, had underestimated the Lord by 7,000 percent. We're not truly honest about our burdens if we don't take into account the sovereignty of God.

Dr. Jay Kesler, president emeritus of Taylor University, wrote,

Many of us got the idea in the 1960s that you should be true to your emotions, that you should feel free to express them regardless of the situation. . . . There's a kernel of truth in that idea, but things just aren't that simple for leaders, who always have to consider the impact of what they say and do on those who follow. . . . In my case as a college president, for example, I've found that if I go public with discouragement, the whole campus goes down. If someone asks me how I'm feeling and I say, "Oh, I'm really kind of down today," before long little groups are getting together all over the place and saying, "Jay's discouraged." And if Jay's discouraged, they seem to think, something must really be wrong.

Consequently, I've learned to stay up, to be encouraging. I save my negativity for the small group of people who can handle it, because the larger group can't do anything about the situation anyway. They need leadership. It's not deception or subterfuge to be optimistic, to be excited, to encourage others to believe in God; it's just one of the elements needed in a leader.[15]

It took me a long time to learn how contagious our attitudes were to others. Pleasantly productive leaders harness the power of biblical joy. It can't be faked, but it can be cultivated. It isn't optional; it's indispensible. To be joyfully thankful is the foundation of influence. A happy heart makes a cheerful face; a cheerful heart has a continual feast; and a cheerful look brings joy to the hearts of others. That's executive joy, and that creates the environment for effective leadership.

In summary:

Proverbs 15:13: *"A happy heart makes a cheerful face."* That's *transforming* joy. It is personality-altering. It involves the attitudes we choose to cultivate inside us. While others seek transient pleasure, the joy of the Lord is transformative to our personalities and to our leadership potential, even transforming the expressions on our faces.

Proverbs 15:15: *"A cheerful heart has a continual feast."* That's *transcendent* joy. Biblical joy turns every day into an adventure. Cheerful people enjoy life more than others, even if they aren't as well off in wealth or rank (see verses 16–17). That gives us an authentic attitudinal basis for leadership.

Proverbs 15:30: "A cheerful look brings joy to the heart of others." That's *transferable* joy. When we convey cheerfulness in the way we interact with others, it spreads joy to someone else. That's the essence of leadership.

The believer who is in a healthy state
rejoices mainly in God Himself.
He is happy because there is a God,
and because God, in His person and character, is what He is.
All the attributes of God become continual sources of joy
to the thoughtful, contemplative believer.

—Charles Haddon Spurgeon, in his sermon "The Joy of the Lord."[1]

22

Well Versed in Happiness

While Benjamin Franklin was living in England on behalf of the American colonies, he received word that two of his friends had died—Stephen Potts and William Parsons. Both belonged to a club Franklin had organized years before. Pondering the news, Franklin thought of the contrast in the personalities of the two men. Parsons was always fretting in the midst of prosperity, whereas Potts was always laughing in the midst of poverty. "It seems, then," observed the analytical Franklin, "that happiness in this life rather depends on internals than externals; and that, besides the natural effects of wisdom and virtue, vice and folly, there is such a thing as being of a happy or an unhappy constitution."[2]

Happiness *does* depend on internals and it has much to do with the constitution of the soul. It has little to do with circumstances, wealth, fame, or age. It may have something to do with brain chemistry, but maybe not as much as the experts claim. Joy is not an inherited trait, though our genetic dispositions and childhood environments influence the formation of our attitudes. It's not just a matter of personality or temperament, though we're all made differently. The thing that makes some people happier is that they have found something to be substantially happy about, and they have learned to cultivate that attitude like a farmer tending prize-winning crops.

Whatever our inborn traits, we can shape our dispositions with the right spiritual truths and tools. We can become better. We can grow happier. Joy requires a spiritual foundation, grounded in truth and centered on Christ. There's no joy without Jesus—at least, not the kind of joy the Bible portrays. But even dedicated Christians need help sustaining their joy in this woeful world. For me, the turning point came in discovering the fifteen verses I mentioned in the previous chapter.

In an earlier chapter I referred to Ezra, "a teacher well versed in the Law of Moses" (Ezra 7:6). In emulating his example, we must be well versed in what the Bible says about joy. The single best way to maintain a joyful attitude is to have a rich handful of *joy* verses, which we learn by heart, quote frequently, and ponder often. Taken seriously, these verses can shape our psyche:

> Restoring the art of Scripture memory is crucial for us, our churches, and children. It's vital for mental and emotional health and for spiritual wellbeing. Though it's as easy as repeating words aloud, it's as powerful as acorns dropping into furrows in the forest. It makes the Bible portable; you can take it with you everywhere without packing it in purse or briefcase. It makes Scripture accessible day and night. It allows God's words to sink into your brain and permeate your subconscious and even your unconscious thoughts. It gives you a word to say to anyone, in season and out of season. It fills your heart and home with the best thoughts ever recorded. It saturates the personality, satiates the soul, and stockpiles the mind. It changes the atmosphere of every family and alters the weather forecast of every day.[3]

Psalm 19:8 says, "The precepts of the Lord are right, giving *joy* to the heart."[4] When we memorize verses about the joy of the Lord, it's like implanting radioactive truth into the core of our personalities. God's Word is nutritional therapy for happy hearts. We find His words—key verses, especially on the subject of joy—and eat them, chew on them, digest them, and they're assimilated through our systems, conveying joy to every cell of the soul.

Here, then, are some verses to chew on, which I'm listing and quoting below with a few observations about each. Select some of these and commit them to memory. Find one to quote aloud every morning and evening for the next month. Post it on your dashboard or desk. I'm confident in the power of Scripture. I'm certain these verses will yield bushels of joy when memorized, internalized, and personalized. It's the best way I know to be well versed in happiness.

Psalm 100:2: "Serve the Lord with gladness."[5] Psalm 100 was affectionately called the Old Hundredth by the Puritans. It's short— only five verses—but as uplifting as any passage in the Bible. It begins by telling us to make a joyful noise to the Lord—to shout joyfully to Him—and to serve Him with gladness. Sometimes we serve the Lord out of duty, drudgery, and determination, but not with joy. Yet another passage—Deuteronomy 28:47–48—carries a sober warning about that: "Because you did not serve the Lord your God joyfully and gladly in the time of prosperity, therefore in hunger and thirst, in nakedness and dire poverty, you will serve the enemies the Lord sends against you." That's a jolting passage! It's not enough to serve the Lord. It's not even enough to serve Him faithfully and earnestly. We must serve Him with gladness and come into His presence with singing. Commentator Matthew Henry called joy the "oil on the wheels of our obedience."[6] A joyful Savior is best served by joyful servants who are going about His business and finishing the work He's given them—with joy!

Proverbs 17:22: "A cheerful heart is good medicine." Joy is the wonder drug of the heart. We occasionally need antibiotics or antiseptics to stay physically well, and we need cheerfulness to maintain our mental health. People without the joy of the Lord need divine hospitalization. Their energy is depleted, their strength has ebbed, their complexions are hollow, and they're susceptible to spiritual infection. The Great Physician has an antidote: A cheerful heart is good medicine.

Romans 15:13: "May the God of hope fill you with all joy and peace as you trust in him, so that you may overflow with hope by the power of the Holy Spirit." This verse conveys Paul's benediction for the church at Rome as he neared the end of his great epistle. He referred to our Lord as the "God of hope," indicating God is always optimistic, always positive, and always confident of the future. The Lord pours His joy and peace into us like wine into a goblet. By trusting Him with our concerns, we're availing ourselves of His joy and peace, which are described here as liquid attitudes. They don't drip or dribble into our hearts; they flood our souls with the Holy Spirit. The result—an overflowing life, a life that blesses others. The joy of Jesus is a spring that never runs dry.

Nehemiah 8:10: "This day is holy to our Lord. Do not grieve, for the joy of the Lord is your strength." The book of Nehemiah involves the rebuilding of the defensive walls around Jerusalem. The project is described in the first chapters of the book and completed in chapter 6. Nehemiah planned a great day of celebration to dedicate the reconstructed walls to the Lord, and that happened in chapter 12. In the interim, between the completion and the dedication of the walls, Ezra and Nehemiah held a great citywide Bible conference, which is described in chapter 8. Everyone in Jerusalem assembled in a square near one of the gates, and Ezra stood and read the Scripture, explained it, and gave the application. As the people heard the Law, they were saddened, for it had been so long neglected among them. But Nehemiah and Ezra told them to cheer up, to celebrate, to eat and drink and rejoice, for this was a holy day to the Lord: "Do not grieve, for the joy of the Lord is your strength."

That's my favorite phrase in the whole Bible on the subject of joy. The joy of the Lord gives us energy. It fuels our optimism and provides our stamina. It keeps us strong against our enemies and steady in the face of adversity. The joy of the Lord is our stability, our vitality, our muscle, and our might. The joy of the Lord is the strength of our lives.

Psalm 118:24: "This is the day the Lord has made; we will rejoice and be glad in it." From its opening to its close, Psalm 118 brims with a victorious sense of joy. It's defiant and intrepid in attitude, and its core message is about the coming Messiah—the stone the builders rejected, who nevertheless is the Cornerstone (verse 22). "The Lord has done this"—done everything for us in Christ, who is the Cornerstone of our lives—"and it is marvelous in our eyes" (verse 23). So we'll never face a morning we cannot begin with these words: "This is the day the Lord has made; let us rejoice and be glad in it" (verse 24).

Philippians 4:4: "Rejoice in the Lord always. I will say it again: Rejoice!" The letter to the Philippians is Paul's epistle of joy. Though he was imprisoned and writing from a dank cell, his spirit was unsinkable and irrepressible. If you're ever in low spirits and need a simple therapeutic Bible study, read through the four chapters of Philippians with a colored pencil and highlight every reference to joy and rejoicing. It's summed up in chapter 4, when Paul gives a series of bullet-pointed instructions regarding inner peace:

- Rejoice and rejoice some more (verse 4).

- Be gentle with others (verse 5a).

- Remember the nearness of the Lord (verse 5b).

- Don't worry about anything but pray about everything, with thanksgiving (verse 6).

- Meditate on what is excellent and praiseworthy (verses 8–9).

- If you do these things, the peace of God will guard you and the God of peace will guide you (verses 7, 9).

John 15:11: "I have told you this so that my joy may be in you and that your joy may be complete." After covering the three-year ministry of Jesus in twelve chapters, John suddenly slows his narrative and devotes the next five chapters—John 13–17—to a period of time that probably didn't exceed three hours. These chapters recount the Upper Room Discourse, where Jesus said, "Do not let your hearts be troubled" (John 14:1). This is the last time He met with His followers before being arrested and crucified, and His words are so poignant we can't read them without feeling we are there listening to Him. Though the atmosphere was tense and the disciples frightened, Jesus spoke of peace, joy, mansions in heaven, the coming of the Comforter, the power of answered prayer, and the reality of His own dimensions of joy. Because He spoke these words on the worst night of His life, they are in full effect on even the worst days of ours. As the Amplified Bible puts it: "I have told you these things, that My joy and delight may be in you; and that your joy and gladness may be of full measure and complete and over-flowing."

John 17:13: "I am coming to you now, but I say these things while I am still in the world, so that they may have the full measure of my joy within them." After Jesus concluded His Upper Room Discourse in John 13–16, He offered the greatest prayer in the Bible—His High Priestly Prayer in John 17, for all His followers, including you and me (see John 17:20). In this prayer He affirmed the power of His teachings, telling the Father He was leaving behind words that would reproduce in His followers "the full measure of my joy."

What is the full measure of Christ's joy? If you could take all the joy that belongs to Jesus and pour it into an immense basin and measure it, how many gallons would it represent? If you could stretch it out like a highway and gauge it with an odometer, how many miles would it cover? If you could suspend it like a beam of light through the heavens and measure it with an infinite tape measure, how tall would it be? Whatever those measurements, that's the amount of joy God wants us to experience. That's why Peter called it "unspeakable" . . .

1 Peter 1:8: "Joy unspeakable and full of glory."[7] Another translation says: "Although you don't yet see Him, you do believe in Him and celebrate with a joy that is glorious and beyond words."[8]

Psalm 51:12: "Restore to me the joy of your salvation." Psalm 51 is King David's prayer of repentance after the adulterous affair and murder conspiracy that nearly wrecked his life and reign. For an entire year he lost all his joy in life. Sin steals away our joy like a swindler. As evangelist Billy Sunday said, "If there is no joy in religion, you have got a leak in your religion."[9] When David finally confessed and repented as recorded in Psalm 51, he asked God to create in him a clean heart, to renew a right spirit within him, to renew his experience with the Holy Spirit, and to restore joy to his soul. Personal revival is essentially a revival of joy, as we also see in Psalm 85:6: "Will you not revive us again, that your people may rejoice in you?"

It's impossible to be pleasant or productive without the joy of the Lord. As Helen Keller said, "Joy is the holy fire that keeps our purpose warm and our intelligence aglow. Resolve to keep happy, and your joy and you shall form an invincible host against difficulty."[10]

The ocean of God's joy is an unsinkable sea. It's as uplifting as the heart of Jesus. If joy isn't yet a habitual pattern for you, learn to remind yourself every day of the verses God has given, the Spirit He has bestowed, the blessings He offers, the future He envisions, and the promises He provides. Begin to rejoice in the Lord at once; and I will say it again: Rejoice!

Just for the "joy" of it, I've listed a few more verses below:

- **Galatians 5:22:** But the fruit of the Spirit is . . . joy.

- **Romans 14:17–18:** The kingdom of God is not a matter of eating and drinking, but of righteousness, peace, and joy in the Holy Spirit, because anyone who serves Christ in this way is pleasing to God and receives human approval.

- **John 20:20:** The disciples were overjoyed when they saw the Lord.

- **Luke 10:20:** Do not rejoice that the spirits submit to you, but rejoice that your names are written in heaven.

- **Psalm 126:3:** The Lord has done great things for us, and we are filled with joy.

- **Psalm 16:11:** You make known to me the path of life; you will fill me with joy in Your presence.

- **Isaiah 55:12:** You will go out in joy and be led forth in peace; the mountains and hills will burst into song before you.

- **Psalm 94:19:** When anxiety was great within me, your consolation brought me joy.

- **Romans 12:12:** Be joyful in hope, patient in affection, faithful in prayer.

- **James 1:2–3:** Consider it pure joy, my brothers and sisters, whenever you face trials of many kinds, because you know that the testing of your faith produces perseverance.

Study Questions for Mastering This Pattern

1. What aspect of the biblical teachings on joy in this segment of *Mastering Life* most surprised you?

_____

_____

_____

_____

2. How often is the joy of the Lord reflected in your daily attitudes and countenance?

_____

_____

_____

_____

3. Who in your life is most influenced by your attitudes? In general terms, does your disposition help or hinder the atmospherics of your relationships?

_____

_____

_____

_____

_____

4. When the Bible says the cheerful heart "has a continual feast," what does that mean in literal and practical terms?

_____

_____

_____

_____

5. Which of the verses in this chapter most impressed you? How soon do you think you could memorize it and make it your own?

_____

_____

_____

_____

For more help in applying these principles or for group study or staff training, download my free *Mastering Life Workbook* at RobertJMorgan.com/MasteringLifeWorkbook.

THE NINTH PATTERN

Practice the Power of Plodding

Is your place a small place?
Tend it with care!—
He set you there.
Is your place a large place?
Guard it with care!—
He set you there.
Whate'er your place, it is
Not yours alone, but His
Who set you there.

—John Oxenham[1]

23

Don't Despise the
Day of Small Things

Anthony Trollope was a nineteenth-century writer known for his prolific accomplishments, including reforming the British postal service by introducing pillar boxes so people could easily mail letters. His novels are popular to this day and his influence is lasting. Trollope summarized the secret of his success in one telling sentence: "A small daily task, if it be really daily, will beat the labors of a spasmodic Hercules." In his autobiography, Trollope said he had never fancied himself a man of genius, but he had understood one thing—the power of the water drop to hollow the stone.[2]

Earlier in *Mastering Life Before It's Too Late,* I wrote of God's assigning our work in one-day increments. I'm convinced we're too enamored of the dramatically big when most of life is blessedly small. Sometimes we mistakenly equate smallness with insignificance, but that's an indictment against God's wisdom in planning our ways. I'm not against big moments; I relish them. There's nothing wrong with envisioning large dreams and planning outsize efforts. To some people it comes naturally; it's a gift. Daniel 11:32 says, "The people who know their God shall be strong and carry out great exploits."[3] But God's exploits aren't always theatrical, and the Bible warns against despising the day of small things.

Where do we find that phrase in Scripture? It occurs in the latter part of Old Testament times. In 587 BC, the city of Jerusalem was destroyed by Babylonian invaders who reduced the Lord's glorious temple to a pile of smoldering rubble. The survivors were marched into exile hundreds of miles away, and strangers and stragglers inhabited the ruins of the Holy City. Decades later, a remnant of Jewish exiles returned to try to rebuild Solomon's great temple, but they didn't have Solomon's resources. They didn't have his army of engineers, architects, and laborers, nor his wealth and capital. They found themselves in a hostile environment, and their efforts were criticized by local foes.

After clearing away the debris and reassembling the foundation, many of the older exiles wept, remembering the original temple in its splendor. By contrast, their present work seemed small, underfunded, and insubstantial. As opposition increased and morale decreased, the work came to a halt. For many years the construction site was abandoned. Then two preachers rose up with fresh wind and fire—Haggai and Zechariah. We number these men among the "minor" prophets, but their messages conveyed maximum truth that has stood the test of time.

In one of his sermons, Haggai asked the exiles: "Who of you is left who saw this house in its former glory? How does it look to you now? Does it not seem to you like nothing?" Then he relayed God's message to them: " 'But now be strong . . . be strong . . . be strong, all you people of the land, . . . and work. For I am with you,' declares the Lord Almighty . . . 'My Spirit remains among you. Do not fear.' " (2:3–5).

Haggai went on to convey an amazing promise from God:

This is what the Lord Almighty says: "In a little while I will once more shake the heavens and the earth, the sea and the dry land. I will shake all nations, and what is desired by all nations will come, and I will fill this house with glory. . . . The glory of this present house will be greater than the glory of the former house." (Haggai 2:6–7, 9)

In other words, the Lord said: "Does this task seem so insignificant? One day I'll shake up history, and the One desired by nations—the Messiah—will come. He will stand in this very temple, which will be an arena for His ministry. You're building this structure for Him, and its future glory will exceed anything Solomon imagined."

As history unfolded, that's exactly what happened.

Haggai's fellow prophet, Zechariah, had a similar message: " 'Not by might nor by power, but by My Spirit,' says the Lord Almighty . . . 'Who dares despise the day of small things?' " (Zechariah 4:6, 10). Though the remnant was weak, their efforts small, and their building inferior, the Holy Spirit was there in ways they couldn't see. Their plodding efforts would achieve great results, recorded in God's logbook of history. Those lugging one stone atop another in 520 BC felt their bodies bathed in sweat and their eyes with tears. But from God's perspective, they were doing the greatest work in the world in paving the way for the Savior, and their true success wouldn't be fully realized for a half-millennium.

You've got to take it one game at a time, one hitter at a time. You've got to go on doing the things you've talked about and agreed about beforehand. You can't get three outs at a time or five runs at a time. You've got to concentrate on each play, each hitter, each pitch. All this makes the game much slower and much clearer. It breaks it down to its smallest part. If you take the game like that—one pitch, one hitter, one inning at a time, and then one game at a time—the next thing you know, you look up and you've won.[4]

—Baseball legend Rick Dempsey

Life has a cumulative effect; it compounds constantly. There's no way to know the ripple effect of our labor when patiently, ploddingly pursued. We finish years by completing days, and we consummate days by seizing moments. We complete major tasks through small, persistent increments . It's said we overestimate what we can do in ten days but underestimate what we can do in ten years. When we take care of the days, the Lord will take care of the years.

This is plodding. It's easier to *plot* than to *plod*, but both are necessary. In hiking a rugged route, we have to plan our course, but then it's a matter of putting one foot in front of another—thousands of times. We keep at it until the trip becomes a memory preparing us for the next expedition. It's possible to be so concerned about great things, we fail to enjoy the little steps that are truly great. The little tasks we accomplish are often greater than the big ones we envision, and in any event, they're the stuff from which a lasting legacy is composed.

Speaking of hiking, while on a speaking engagement last month in California, I spent an afternoon at Calaveras Big Trees State Park near Yosemite. I was awestruck by the giant sequoias, which are ancient—some of the trees I saw were there when David fought Goliath and when Jesus stilled the storms. Photographs of these gigantic trees can't capture their true size, and I can't describe them. I felt like a little person among giants. At one of the Sequoias, there was a display about their pinecones, and the caption at the top of the display read: "The Small World of a Big Tree." Each giant sequoia may have as many as forty thousand cones at once, and each contains an entire world of living organisms. Every cone is a miniature planet populated by tiny creatures at home in the heights, who make the forest function as it should and allow the trees to reproduce. In God's economy, the pinecone and its tiny residents are as wonderfully made, and as vital, as the towering trees that command our attention. In His will, there are no tiny tasks and no small creatures.

Earlier I referred to my friend Tom Tipton. He stood at the Lincoln Memorial with Dr. Martin Luther King Jr. He still boasts of being in charge of all the toilets that day. Later he stood alongside Hubert Humphrey in the political arena. He sang in great arenas, before huge crowds, on nationwide television, and in corridors of power. Now older and feebler, he enjoys visiting nursing homes and singing for the residents. He told me the joy of singing at retirement homes was as great an honor as singing in the White House, for it represents the will of God at this stage in his life.

That kind of attitude takes the pressure off always having to find significance in big things and success in big numbers. French Jesuit Father Jean Nicolas Grou wrote:

> Little things come daily, hourly, within our reach, and they are no less calculated to set forward our growth in holiness than are the greater occasions which occur but rarely. Moreover, fidelity in trifles, and an earnest seeking to please God in little matters, is a test of real devotion and love. Let your aim be to please our dear Lord perfectly in little things.[5]

Moses told the Israelites, "The Lord your God will drive out those nations before you, little by little. You will not be allowed to eliminate them all at once, or the wild animals will multiply around you" (Deuteronomy 7:22). Along the same lines, Proverbs 13:11 says, "Whoever gathers money little by little makes it grow." Most of our accomplishments occur little by little, day by day, step by step, here a little and there a little. Jesus told us to be faithful in little things, for those who are faithful in little are faithful in much. That's the motto of the Mount School in York, England, a boarding school for teenage girls started by the Quakers in 1831. The school slogan is *Fidelis in Parvo*, another Latin phrase, meaning "faithfulness in little things."

Patient plodding produces durable results. When we give up on a project, we waste the labor and time already expended. Admittedly, there are times when we realize a task or a project isn't worth the effort and we abandon it. There's no reason, after all, to throw good time after bad. But successful people rarely face that dilemma because: 1.) they learn to count the cost in advance and to tackle only worthwhile projects that reasonably represent God's will; and 2.) they're not easily discouraged and seldom capitulate in tough times.

The Bible is chock-full of commands and promises to galvanize us against discouragement when times are tough and tasks seem futile. The Lord told Joshua to conquer the Promised Land one footstep at a time: "I will give you every place where you set your foot . . . Do not be discouraged, for the Lord your God will be with you wherever you go" (Joshua 1:3, 9). The Bible says, "Be strong and courageous, and do the work. Do not be afraid or discouraged, for the Lord God, my God, is with you. He will not fail you or forsake you until all the work for the service of the temple of the Lord is finished" (1 Chronicles 28:20).

That's good advice whatever the setting. Most companies begin with a good idea, a small investment, and lots of faithful work over long periods of time. That's how careers are forged, relationships built, crops grown, and ministries established. Almost everything starts small, and sometimes it stays small; but when it's dedicated to the Lord, the results are always magnified by grace. That's why Proverbs 16:3 says, "Commit to the Lord whatever you do, and he will establish your plans."

Appreciating smallness doesn't mean settling for mediocrity, downsizing our dreams, or allowing our vision to sink to the lowest denominator. But *size* doesn't matter as much as we think, whereas *service* matters more than we realize. The Son of Man came not to be served, but to serve; and true fulfillment is found in the will of God—nothing more and nothing less.

Missionary William Carey is a prime example. He was born in an obscure English village in the 1700s. As a child, he was sickly, afflicted by numerous allergies, and sensitive to the sun. He was also poorly educated. Entering adolescence, William frequently got into trouble. He married, but his wife developed mental illness. He contracted a dread disease that left him entirely bald. He was the town cobbler, but his business failed. He tried teaching school but didn't succeed. He pastored a church, but his sermons weren't well received. He developed a passion for overseas missions and felt God calling him to go abroad, but his fellow ministers were opposed. When he did make it to India, his wife lost her mind, his coworker mishandled their funds, and he encountered a thousand obstacles.

But fast-forward to the end of the story. William Carey labored faithfully in India for forty-one years, dying there at age seventy-three. When all was said and done, as his biographer points out, he had translated the complete Bible into six languages, and portions of the Bible into twenty-nine others. He had founded over one hundred rural schools for the people of India. He had established Serampore College, which is still training ministers to this day. He had introduced the concept of a savings bank to the farmers of India. He had published the first Indian newspaper. He had written dictionaries and grammars in five different languages. He had so influenced the nation of India that, largely through his efforts, the practice of suttee (the burning of living widows with the corpses of their dead husbands) was outlawed. Additionally, he launched the modern era of missions and laid the foundations for the modern science of missiology. As Mary Drewery wrote in her gripping account of Carey's life, "The number of actual conversions attributed to him is pathetically small; the number indirectly attributable to him must be legion."[6]

What was his secret? Carey's sister summarized it like this:

"Whatever he began he finished: difficulties never seemed to discourage his mind." His brother Thomas wrote, "I . . . recollect that he was, from a boy . . . always resolutely determined never to give up any point or particle of anything on which his mind was set." Carey himself once put it this way in a letter to his nephew: "Eustace, if after my removal any one should think it worth his while to write my *Life*, I will give you a criterion by which you may judge of its correctness. If he give me credit for being a plodder, he will describe me justly. I can plod. I can persevere in any definite pursuit. To this I owe everything."[7]

There are grave difficulties on every hand and more
are looming ahead. Therefore we must go forward.

—William Carey

The word *plod* comes from an Old English word meaning "puddle."[8] A plodder is someone willing to get his feet wet and wade through the mud and mire to arrive at his destination. "By perseverance," said Charles Spurgeon, "the snail reached the ark."[9]

The quality of perseverance is at the core of character. The "Love" chapter of the Bible, 1 Corinthians 13, says, "Love . . . always perseveres" (verse 7). Paul told Timothy to persevere in both life and doctrine, for in so doing he would save both himself and his hearers (1 Timothy 4:16). The writer of Hebrews said, "You need to persevere" (10:36). James said, "Blessed is the one who perseveres until trial . . . As you know, we count as blessed those who have persevered" (James 1:12, 5:11). According to Romans 5 and James 1, the Lord allows pressures into our lives just to develop the quality of perseverance, for it's the mark of maturity.

Hebrews 12:1 commands us to "run with perseverance the race marked out for us." In my daily devotional book *All to Jesus,* I told of a Cuban mail carrier named Felix Carvajal, who decided to enter the 1904 Olympics in St. Louis and win the marathon for his country. He had no money or backing, but, quitting his job, he managed to catch a boat to New Orleans and hitchhike to St. Louis, where the American team took pity on him and gave him food and a bed. Felix had neither uniform nor running shoes. He didn't have training or experience. Cutting off his pants above the knees, he appeared at the starting line in street shoes. The heat was withering and the humidity was oppressive. Most of the runners collapsed, and one nearly died. But being from Cuba, Felix was right at home with the heat and humidity. He laughed, joked, and talked all the way until he was within two miles of the finish. He was far ahead of all challengers.

That's when he spotted an orchard alongside the road and stopped to eat an apple. He was hungry enough to eat several of the green apples, and suddenly Felix doubled over with stomach cramps and could only watch as three men overtook him. Of the thirty-one starters that day, only fourteen finished the race. Felix came in fourth; he should have been first, but he stopped too soon.[10]

Dr. V. Raymond Edman, president of my alma mater, Wheaton College, was famous for his slogan *It's always too soon to quit.* If we're involved in big things, they're big enough for God to handle. If we're involved in small things, they're not too small for Him to bless. Our lives do not consist in the abundance of money, fame, prestige, popularity, plaques, or accomplishments, but in being pleasantly productive in tasks great and small, doing them faithfully, in increments, with joy, and seeing the work through to the finish line. Remember what Jesus prayed in John 17:4: "I have brought you glory on earth by finishing the work you gave me to do."

Success is doing our work one task at a time, one step at a time, one moment at a time, relishing the smallness of it while trusting

God for its power to change the world through chain reactions of blessings we'll recognize only in heaven. So we must practice the power of plodding and despise not the day of small things.

Sometimes I grow discouraged and wonder if I'm doing any good at all. Statistics fluctuate, and they can determine my mood if I'm not careful. Times change. Tides ebb and flow. Occasionally I see a few results from my work; often I don't. But just as we walk by faith and not by sight, we work that way too. So I fortify myself with God's Word— often from verses in the minor prophets like Haggai and Zechariah— and press onward, cheerfully. The apostle Paul said, "One thing I do: Forgetting what is behind and straining toward what is ahead, I press on toward the goal to win the prize for which God has called me heavenward in Christ Jesus. All of us, then, who are mature should take such a view of things" (Philippians 3:14–15).

Our lives and labors call for prayerful perseverance, patience persistence, and plodding. If God has assigned our daily tasks, He'll produce an eternal harvest. Don't give up; and don't worry if the work seems small, the costs large, or the results meager. When we go about our Father's business, whatever it is, He creates through us a ripple effect stretching to the shores of eternity. Only in heaven can we calculate the sum total of the impact of our lives. But, in the process, we can show the world what it means to be pleasantly productive people. As Dante Alighieri said in *The Divine Comedy*: "*E 'n la sua volontade è nostra pace*"—"In His will is peace."[11]

> *Therefore, my dear brothers and sisters, stand firm.*
> *Let nothing move you. Always give yourselves*
> *fully to the work of the Lord,*
> *because you know that your labor*
> *in the Lord is not in vain.*
> —1 Corinthians 15:58

Study Questions for Mastering This Pattern

1. Do you ever struggle with a sense of insignificance or envy? How can the biblical truths in this chapter dispel those temptations?

_____

_____

_____

_____

2. Think of the greatest beneficial influences in your life. Can you trace them back to their sources? How far back can you trace the series of events that brought these good influences into your life?

_____

_____

_____

_____

3. Why is discouragement an invalid attitude for Christian servants?

_____

_____

_____

_____

4. What small things are you most thankful for?

_____

_____

_____

_____

5. Are you tired of the grind? Is it because it's time to step away from it, or do you need to rededicate yourself to seeing it through?

_____

_____

_____

_____

For more help in applying these principles or for group study or staff training, download my free *Mastering Life Workbook* at RobertJMorgan.com/MasteringLifeWorkbook.

THE TENTH PATTERN

Remember There Are Two of You

I am the Vine, you are the branches.
When you're joined with me and I with you,
the relation intimate and organic,
the harvest is sure to be abundant.
Separated, you can't produce a thing.

—John 14:5[1]

24

Double Vision

In 1961, an executive in Amsterdam named Thomas van Beek recruited a capable assistant to help him master and manage his work. Miss Neef came with excellent references, a good grasp of typing and shorthand, and a reservoir of perpetual energy. She handled calls with proficiency, paperwork with competence, and emergencies with calm. Even when van Beek and his colleagues drooped from exhaustion at the end of long days, Miss Neef seemed indefatigable. She was a one-woman miracle, and for twelve years she managed the office with machine-like efficiency.

Finally the dreaded day came when Miss Neef turned in her notice. She was ready to retire, and no one could dissuade her. It wasn't a matter of long hours or low pay; she simply longed for the next chapter in her life. With reluctance, Mr. van Beek planned a retirement party for this remarkable woman who had invested years doing the work of two people without complaining.

That's when the surprise came out. To the wonderment of all, Miss Neef arrived at the party with another person—another Miss Neef! For a dozen years, two sisters, identical twins, had been sharing the same job, each working half-time, rotating in and out according to their own covert schedule and splitting the paycheck between them.[2] As coworkers did a double take, the Misses Neef smiled at the success of their charade, having double-teamed their colleagues for over a decade.

As I read that story I thought of another anecdote tucked away in my files. It involves a conversation between two renowned men of yesteryear, missionary and explorer David Livingstone and British preacher and author Charles Haddon Spurgeon. The latter was famous for the unbelievable quantity of his work—preaching multiple times to vast crowds every week, pastoring the largest church in London, producing books and magazines faster than anyone could read them, and heading up dozens of charitable and humanitarian organizations. Livingstone asked him, "How do you manage to do two men's work in a single day?"

Spurgeon had a simple reply: "You have forgotten that there are two of us." He went on to explain that he had an unseen Partner, and this Partner was doing most of the work.[3] That's the final principle I want to cover in this book. To be pleasantly productive in life, it's necessary to remember there are two of you. The life you're living and the work you're doing are eternally significant only when it is Jesus living and working through you. That's the upshot of Galatians 2:20: "I have been crucified with Christ and I no longer live, but Christ lives in me. The life I now live in the body, I live by faith in the Son of God, who loved me and gave himself for me."

Jesus Christ lives within His followers through the divine agency of the Holy Spirit. He replicates His qualities through our personalities and accomplishes His purposes through our efforts. We truly master life only when we recognize Jesus Christ as the Unseen Senior Partner in all our pursuits. Whatever our assignment, profession, status, or station in life, it's not a matter of what we're doing *for* Christ but what He does *through* us. This is the one and only means to perpetual and pleasant productivity.

"Abide"

A biblical term that describes our relationship in Christ is "abiding," and John 15 is the "abiding chapter" in the Bible. It's part of the final sermon Jesus gave, spoken on His way to the Garden of Gethsemane on the last night of His natural life. Wending His way through the darkened and deserted streets of Old Jerusalem, leading His clueless disciples from the Upper Room toward Gethsemane, and having only an hour or two remaining with them, Jesus said something unexpected. Perhaps they were passing a little vineyard in someone's backyard. Perhaps in the moonlight He saw the engraving of a cluster of grapes on the portals of massive temple as they passed beneath it. For whatever reason, Jesus began comparing Himself to a grapevine. He described His disciples as branches. With a few well-chosen phrases, He gave us a profound lesson: If we maintain a healthy connection with Him, like a branch attached to a vine, we don't have to *try* to be productive. We cannot *help* being productive. We will bear fruit, He said, more fruit and much fruit, fruit that remains. The Holy Spirit will flow through us like sap circulating between vine and branches to produce a vintage life. Only by abiding in Christ can we actualize the lasting legacy He has designed for us.

What did Jesus mean by "fruit"? In the immediate context, I think He meant the reproduction *within us* of His own attitudes, which are called the Fruit of the Spirit in Galatians 5:22–23: Love, joy, peace, patience, kindness, goodness, faithfulness, gentleness, and self-control. This is a ninefold list of the primary personality traits of Jesus, which He wants to duplicate in His disciples so we'll be like Him. Of course, in those days before the hybridization of seedless grapes, all grapes had seeds, which allowed them to propagate and reproduce. It's the same with the fruit of the Spirit. Whenever we display the attitudes of Christ it paves the way for others to receive the evangelistic witness of the gospel. So the fruit of the Spirit leads to a spiritually reproductive life.

By implication, this means that everything we do in the will of God, as we do it with the attitudes of Christ, is a work that will bring Him glory and serve as a witness to His grace. That's mastering life. That's being truly productive. This is, in a broad sense, the fruit Jesus enjoined among us on His nocturnal trek toward Gethsemane and Calvary.

Our own efforts, taken alone, cannot sustain the needed outcomes. No matter how gifted our personalities, they cannot achieve permanent results. No matter how brilliant our minds, they cannot generate true wisdom. No matter how expansive our vision, we can effect nothing on our own. Jesus said in John 15: "Abide in me, and I in you. As the branch cannot bear fruit by itself, unless it abides in the vine, neither can you, unless you abide in me. I am the vine; you are the branches. Whoever abides in me and I in Him, he it is that bears much fruit, for apart from me you can do nothing."[4]

This critical teaching, spoken in Christ's final hours, provides the basis for subsequent Christian history, Christlike character, effective ministry, and personal fulfillment. When we learn to think in these abiding terms, we're experiencing the Exchanged Life.

That phrase—the *Exchanged Life*—came from the ministry of missionary J. Hudson Taylor. While laboring in China, he nearly broke down under the strain of work and worry, but a friend wrote him a letter about resting and abiding in Christ. Pondering the note, Taylor's attention was drawn to the reality of the vine and branches. It was as though blinders fell from his eyes. Taylor realized that a vine can never be productive through its own efforts. Only by abiding in Christ would he achieve true and lasting fruit. After this discovery, Taylor testified, his work was just as intense as before, but the strain was gone. He was working with an unseen Partner who was responsible for any and all lasting results. It was the Exchanged Life—not I, but Christ![5]

I pondered this recently while visiting a vineyard where I studied the rows of trellises interwoven with grapevines. It was winter, and there were no clusters of grapes, not even leaves. But the branches seemed unconcerned. I listened carefully, but I didn't hear a single branch grunting and groaning and grinding away to bear fruit through its own herculean efforts. They somehow knew that the primary thing was to stay connected to the vine, and in due season the blossoms would appear and the fruit would mature according to natural processes God established at the creation.

In the same way, as I said in an earlier chapter, it's not our *work for* the Lord but our *walk with* the Lord that's most important. It's about keeping our relationship with Him unstained, unstrained, and healthy. As we abide in Christ, the Holy Spirit flows from Him to us and *through* us, bringing about whatever God has for us in its proper season.

"Through"

God's work through us by the Holy Spirit is a life-altering reality that can be traced throughout the New Testament. The historian Luke started his book of Acts by referring to his previous book, the Third Gospel, which was dedicated to a man named Theophilus: "In my former book, Theophilus, I wrote about all that Jesus began to do and to teach until the day he was taken up to heaven" (Acts 1:1–2).

In my Bible I've circled the word *began* in Acts 1:1, because it sets a subtle tone for the rest of the story. The Gospel of Luke doesn't merely tell us what Jesus did and taught, but what He *began* to do and to teach. Luke was thereby implying that now his second book, Acts, would relate what Jesus *continued* to do and to teach, through His people by means of His Spirit. The next chapter, Acts 2, describes how the

Holy Spirit descended on the believers with dramatic phenomena and "came to rest on each of them. All of them were filled with the Holy Spirit" (verses 3–4). The following chapters chronicle the rapid spread of the gospel during the lifetime of the apostles.

Throughout the book of Acts and the letters of Paul, we can track a frequently used preposition—*through*.

- On arriving there, they gathered the church together and reported all that God had done *through* them and how he had opened a door of faith to the Gentiles. (Acts 14:27)

- When they came to Jerusalem, they were welcomed by the church and the apostles and elders, to whom they reported everything God had done *through* them. (Acts 15:4)

- The whole assembly became silent as they listened to Barnabas and Paul telling about the signs and wonders God had done among the Gentiles *through* them. (Acts 15:12)

- God did extraordinary miracles *through* Paul. (Acts 19:11)

- Paul greeted them and reported in detail what God had done among the Gentiles *through* his ministry. (Acts 21:19)

- I will not venture to speak of anything except what Christ has accomplished *through* me. (Romans 15:18)

- We are therefore Christ's ambassadors, as though God were making his appeal *through* us. (2 Corinthians 5:20)

- I can do all this *through* him who gives me strength. (Philippians 4:13)

- The Lord stood at my side and gave me strength, so that *through* me the message might be fully proclaimed and all the Gentiles might hear it. (2 Timothy 4:17)

Now, two millennia later, nothing has changed about God's core methodology. As we saw in earlier chapters, He has preplanned and assigned our work. He knows the impact He wants us to make. He knows the lives He wants us to touch. He knows the good He wants us to do. The truly astounding thing is this: Not only has He prepared our work in advance, He now intends to fulfill it Himself through us by His Spirit as we abide in Christ.

How Do We Do It?

In practical terms, how does this work? Well, in a sense, that's the scope of this entire book with all ten of its core principles, and now is a good time to summarize.

First, we must freely acknowledge the lordship of Christ over every area of life. We must surrender to Him every corner, crevice, and closet. This harkens back to our first principle of devoting ourselves to our Father's business. We have to say,

Lord, I am Yours, lock, stock, and barrel, from top to toe, inside and outside, yesterday, today, and forever. My soul and spirit are Yours. My family and friendships are Yours. My house and land are Yours. My time and talents are Yours. My dollars and cents are yours. So are my problems and pressures. It's all Yours and I'm all Yours. I'm ready to do whatever You tell me and to go wherever You send me.

I'm ready to redeem the time, reorganize my life, clear the decks, and seek first Your kingdom and Your righteousness.

*He died for all, that those who live should
no longer live for themselves but for him who
died for them and was raised again.*

—2 Corinthians 5:15

Second, as we've also seen in prior chapters, we should meet the Lord each morning and as we do so we can ask Him to fill us afresh with His Holy Spirit, even as Ephesians 5:18 commands, "Be filled with the Spirit." The process of being filled with the Spirit means to be under the Spirit's influence and control—singing, being thankful, and being humble (see Ephesians 5:18–21)—and it's an ever-replenishing process. So we should frequently pray, "Lord, may I be filled anew with Your Spirit."

In one of His sermons about prayer, Jesus said, "If you then, though you are evil, know how to give good gifts to your children, how much more will your Father in heaven give the Holy Spirit to those who ask Him!" (Luke 11:13). That's why I offer a simple prayer along these lines every morning during my daily appointment: "Lord, may I be filled with Your Spirit today so that the attitudes and activities of Jesus will overflow from within me like streams of living water."

The hymnist said, "Fill with Thy Spirit 'till all shall see / Christ only, always, living in me."[6] All of life—every moment of every day—should be the overflow of our walk with Him; and all our labor—every effort and every task—should be the overflow of His fullness in us. Psalm 23 says, "My cup overflows" and the writer of Psalm 119:171 adds, "May my lips overflow with praise." Romans 15:13 says, "May the God of hope fill you with all joy and peace as you trust in him, so that you may overflow with hope by the power of the Holy Spirit."

O fill me with Thy fullness, Lord,
Until my very heart overflow,
In kindling thought and glowing word,
Thy love to tell, Thy praise to show.

—Frances Ridley Havergal from her
hymn "Lord, Speak to Me"

Third, we must envision this process in the most realistic terms possible and claim the experience by faith. This harkens back to our "as if" principle. Having surrendered ourselves afresh to the lordship of Christ and having asked for the fullness of His Spirit, we should go into every day *as if* we are under the control and empowerment of the Lord Jesus Himself. This is the life of walking by faith, and, according to the Bible, faith is the victory (1 John 5:4).

It helps to picture this with real mental images. When I walk across a platform to give a talk, for example, I remind myself Jesus is approaching the lectern with me and intends to do the speaking. Obviously, He's not liable for my grammatical goofs, mangled words, or lapses of insight; but He is responsible for the eternal impact of whatever good is done. So I tell myself, *Isn't this strange? I thought I was going to give a talk to this group, but I've now remembered it's not my talk at all. Jesus is here to speak to someone through me, and I'll not know the long-term impact until I get to heaven.*

In the same way we can say:

- *I'm not trying to sign up this new client; Jesus is doing that.* We do our best to present our products or services, but it's the Lord who grants success to our endeavors and gives us favor in the sight of others—or not, depending on what's truly best for us in the long run. In any event, you can visualize Him sitting with you on your side of the table, the unseen person in the room.

- *I'm not raising my child; Jesus is doing it through me.* When we're filled with His love, joy, peace, patience, and wisdom—when His qualities overflow from our personalities into our homes—we're giving our children something priceless.

- *I can't solve this problem; Jesus will give wisdom from above, guide me to the right outcome, and work it all for good.*

- *I'm not trying to control my temper. I'm saying, "Lord, Your patience, please."*

- *I'm not trying to bear this burden. I can cast it in the Lord's hands and claim His peace.*

- *I'm not the one who will save this soul. That's the Lord's part of the work.* We just do our best to share a word of gospel truth or encouragement, knowing He is working through us in ways that may not be immediately visible.

- *I don't have the strength to clean this house, transport this van of kids, prepare this meal, or coach this soccer team.*

*But if this is what the Lord wants me to do today, strength
will rise as I wait upon Him.*

- *I'm not trying to launch this business. I'm saying, "Lord,
as I seek to build my business, I ask Your will to be done
with it, here on earth, just as Your will is done in heaven."*

Major Ian Thomas was a powerful British Bible teacher whose
ministry had a lasting impact on my wife, Katrina, when she was a
young adult in Palm Beach. I went to school with the major's sons,
and through them I became acquainted with his ministry. The great
theme of all his sermons was: Christ in us! Christ, who is our life!

In some of his writings, Major Thomas shared how he came to
appreciate this message. While working in university ministry as a
young man, he nearly collapsed from spiritual exhaustion. He had
labored for seven years with little to show for it, and he was broken
and ready to quit. But one November night in his room, he heard
the Lord's voice—not audibly but almost so: "You see, for seven
years, with utmost sincerity, you have been trying to live for Me, on
My behalf, the life that I have been waiting for seven years to live
through you!"[7]

That moment altered the major's life forever, and the insight
contained in those words launched a lifetime of productivity for the
Savior. This approach to Christianity—full surrender, Spirit-full-
ness, victorious faith—centers on the reality of the indwelling
Christ, who longs to fashion His image within us and accomplish
His designs through us.

Call it the Victorious Christian Life, the Deeper Christian Life,
the Higher Life, the Exchanged Life, the Overcoming Life, the
Overflowing Life, the Life of Faith—all these terms have been used
and, to me, they've never grown trite. I learned the biblical truth behind them while a student at Columbia International University,

have studied them in the writings of the great Keswick preachers and theologians, and have never outlived the usefulness of what I've learned.

We don't journey through life alone, and we can't live the Christian life by ourselves. There are two of us, and whenever I remind myself of that, much of the stress and strain of my work is lifted. Not I, but Christ! Not my strength, but His! Not my glory, but His alone I seek.

One of my favorite writers, nineteenth-century Boston pastor Dr. A. J. Gordon, provided an illustration I've shared many times. While visiting the World's Fair in Chicago, Dr. Gordon saw a man in the distance dressed in colorful, exotic robes. The man was busy pumping water. He appeared to be laboriously turning the crank of a pump and thereby creating a mighty flow of water. Gordon was impressed with the man's energy, his smooth motions, and his obvious physical conditioning. He was pumping a tremendous volume of water. Drawing closer, Gordon was surprised to discover that the man was actually made of wood. Instead of his turning the crank and making the water flow, the flow of water was actually turning the crank and thereby making him go.[8]

Although we're not as impassive as blocks of wood, there is truth in the tale. If we go about our lives and labors in our own energy, always trying to work things up and produce results, we'll wear ourselves out without the desired accomplishments. How much better instead to remember the words Jesus shouted to the passersby at the Festival of Tabernacles in John 7: "'Let anyone who is thirsty come to me and drink. Whoever believes in me, as Scripture has said, rivers of living water will flow from within them.' By this he meant the Spirit, whom those who believed in him were later to receive."[9]

If you're weary or worn out, pull off at a rest stop and pause long enough to double your vision. Remember Galatians 2:20: "Not I but Christ." Only He can successfully live the Christian life. We can't do it by effort or industry, but we can let Him live His life through us by means of His overflowing Spirit as we abide in Christ.

This is the greatest secret to true productivity I've ever known. It's a the core of New Testament truth: Remember, you're not alone. There are two of you.

Galvanize yourself against discouragement;
Treat it as any other sin.
We're doing more than we know,
and in His will we're accomplishing more than we realize.
His multiplication tables go further than our calculators.
His Word doesn't return void,
His promises don't fail,
and our finest work is best pursued by faith.
The true results are His alone,
magnified by grace into glory.

—Robert J. Morgan

25

God's Arithmetic

God is a God of exponential multiplication. When He works through us, the results are astounding. To illustrate the power of God's arithmetic, think of an enormous piece of very thin paper, the kind used by many Bible publishers. If you fold this paper one time, it's two pages thick but still very thin. If you fold it again, it's four pages thick. Fold it again and it's eight pages thick. But mathematicians tell us that if we were to fold this hypothetical piece of paper twenty-five times, it will be about the height of the Empire State Building. If we fold it thirty times, it would reach over six miles into the sky, which is the cruising altitude of jetliners. Fold it forty-five times, and it will reach to the moon. If we fold it ninety-four times, it'll reach across the entire known universe. [1,2]

That is the power of exponential multiplication. This is God's mathematics. When He works through us by His Spirit, He takes our words and works, folds them over, and blesses them. They may be as thin as Bible paper. They may be small in the sight of others. But their impact is like the ripple of a pond that expands through time in increasingly wide circles until it reaches the shores of eternity.

When we accomplish a task assigned us—when we perform a deed, speak a word, pray for a friend, train up a child, tutor a youngster, distribute a Bible, share a testimony, teach a lesson, or support a ministry—we never know the chain reaction God will begin. We can't imagine the cumulative effect of our simple act, influence, or word. That's why the Bible says, "Let us not become weary in doing good, for at the proper time we will reap a harvest if we do not give up" (Galatians 6:9). The Bible frequently reminds us of the principle of sowing and reaping. By its very nature, a harvest is God's method of multiplication. A single seed has the capacity of feeding millions through endless cycles of proliferation. An entire forest resides in an acorn's cup.

In the same way, as we go through life sowing words, deeds, and influence—even if some are no bigger than mustard seeds—the number of people whom Christ can influence through us is incalculable. This is God's arithmetic.

When God created the world, He invented mathematics, and God's fingerprints are all over the world of numbers. Someone said there might be a lot of atheists among scientists, but comparatively few among mathematicians. This world is not random; it's well ordered with unchanging tables of mathematical equations that are rational and constant and absolute. There's especially something intriguing about exponential math. Here God deals in higher powers.

In kindergarten we learned the numbers one through ten, the simplest digits in arithmetic. Add them together and you get 55. But now try multiplying them: $1 \times 2 \times 3 \times 4 \times 5 \times 6 \times 7 \times 8 \times 9 \times 10$. The total comes to 3,628,800.

We might think we're influencing people one by one and little by little, but God knows how to turn our addition into His multiplication, and His calculus is incalculable. Consider the great revival now sweeping China—millions upon millions of people are streaming into the kingdom. Much of what's happening is the by-product of a few words by a fifteen-year-old girl, whose name we don't know and who probably never knew what she had wrought.

I want to tell you the story of the influence she exerted on John Sung, who was born in 1901 into a Methodist preacher's family in

China. As a boy, John helped his father in the ministry and earned the nickname Little Pastor. But John's main interests were intellectual, not spiritual. He was brilliant, always at the top of his class. As a young man he came to America in pursuit of degrees. He earned a PhD at Ohio State University, where you can still find his chemistry essays and research documents in the university library. He is reportedly the first national Chinese to earn a PhD in America.

Along the way, John got away from the Lord and lost his way in life. In the course of time, trying to regain his bearings, he enrolled in New York's Union Theological Seminary, which espouses a very liberal theology. This was the modernist world of Dr. Henry Sloane Coffin and Dr. Harry Emerson Fosdick. In this faithless environment, John Sung became so confused he no longer knew what he believed or why. He grew depressed and was unable to eat or sleep.

One day during the Christmas season, a friend invited him to an evangelistic meeting where Dr. I. M. Haldeman, a brilliant New York City pastor, was scheduled to speak. Arriving at the meeting, John was disappointed to learn the program had changed. Dr. Haldeman wasn't there. Instead, a fifteen-year-old girl, dressed in white and clasping a small Bible, rose to say a few words. John lost interest in the meeting but, unable to exit gracefully, he stayed. The girl read a few verses about the power of the Cross and gave a few words of testimony. That's all, but that was enough. Her few sentences fell into John's heart like seeds ready to burst into life. Shortly thereafter, John embraced Christ as his Lord and Savior and began sharing the news with everyone.

The administration of Union Theological Seminary, thinking him mad, committed him to an insane asylum. He spent six months there, read the Bible cover to cover forty times, and considered the asylum a better seminary than Union.

He was finally released on the condition he would return to

China, and he arrived in Shanghai in the fall of 1927. He started preaching the moment he arrived, and more than 100,000 people were saved during his ministry. He was called the "John Wesley of China." He preached for fifteen years until he died at age forty-three from tuberculosis, but he paved the way for the explosive growth that China is experiencing today.[3]

How many lives are still being changed because of the simple words of a young, white-clad girl through whom Jesus spoke?

Recently, while I was in Europe with Child Evangelism Fellowship, my friend Roy Harrison loaned me a book about the 1859 Irish Revival. I read it with great interest. It told of an English woman named Mrs. Colville, who found Christ as Savior and began to witness to her friends and family. They rejected her testimony and were highly critical of her. In fact, they were so abusive she had to leave home.

Mrs. Colville became a missionary with the Baptist Missionary Society, and under their auspices, she went to the Irish town of Bellymena in November of 1956. She went from door to door sharing her faith. No one listened to her, and she left town in discouragement without a single convert. Or so she thought. In Bellymena, a young man named James McQuilkin had heard her speaking as he sat at a tea table. He rejected her message, but for the next two weeks he had no peace of mind or heart. He finally yielded himself to the Lord Jesus and was wonderfully saved.

McQuilkin began to meet with three other young Irishmen at an old school building, and their prayer was: "Lord, pour out Thy Holy Spirit on this district and country." As a result of that prayer, a revival broke out in Ireland, and it's estimated that approximately 100,000 souls were won to Christ as a result of the visit of a woman who left town thinking her work a failure.[4]

Adding and Multiplying in Acts

In the previous chapter, I mentioned the subtle use of the word *through* in the book of Acts. Now, I'd like to do the same with the words *add* and *multiply*. In the first chapters of Acts, the emphasis is on addition.

- Those who accepted his message were baptized, and about three thousand were *added* to their number that day. (Acts 2:21)

- And the Lord *added* to their number daily those who were being saved. (Acts 2:47)

- More and more men and women believed in the Lord and were *added* to their number. (Acts 5:14)

Beginning in the next chapter, Acts 6, the mathematical term changes to multiplication.

- The number of the disciples was *multiplying*. (Acts 6:1)[5]

- The Word of God spread, and the number of the disciples *multiplied* greatly. (Acts 6:7)[6]

- Then the churches throughout all Judea, Galilee, and Samaria . . . were *multiplied*. (Acts 9:31)

As we've seen, we're assigned our work day by day and we accomplish our tasks one by one. We plod and persevere and sometimes appear to fail. But in God's will, there is no *failure*. We are doing more good than we know. As Christ works through us by His Spirit, He has a way of grasping the plus sign (+) in His omnipotent hand, twisting it a quarter turn, and transforming it into a multiplication sign (×).

You've probably never heard of Ellen Riley, but perhaps you've heard of bestselling writer Eugenia Price. The latter was born in Charleston, West Virginia, where her father was a dentist. Eugenia decided at age ten she wanted to be a writer, and as a young adult she became a successful writer of radio scripts. As an avowed atheist, she had no qualms about filling the growing entertainment appetite of postwar America with whatever content she could sell. But her success didn't bring happiness. "Life is terribly heavy," she wrote, "when you have spent your life convincing yourself and everyone else that you are a success."[7]

Then she ran into a childhood friend, Ellen Riley, who was a Christian. Under Ellen's quiet but persistent witness, Eugenia Price was born again in a New York City hotel room on October 2, 1949. Eugenia soon closed her secular production company and began working in Christian radio programing. She assisted in writing and producing episodes of the Christian broadcast *Unshackled* for the Pacific Garden Mission of Chicago.

In 1953, Eugenia published her first Christian novel. By her death in 1996, she had written fourteen novels, twenty-two inspirational books, and three autobiographies. Her books have sold more than 40 million copies, and most of her novels appeared on the *New York Times* bestseller list. She was a regular speaker at church and civic events. She touched untold millions through radio, the spoken word, and the printed page. And she paved the way for all subsequent Christian fiction writers.[8]

Ellen Riley was undoubtedly excited about winning her childhood friend—a person of one. But she couldn't have imagined how God's multiplication tables would take over.[9]

Over the years I've collected many such stories of how a good deed, an accomplished task, or a forgotten sermon created multiple chain reactions that have influenced human history to this day. I delight in these stories, for they galvanize me against discouragement.

When we are abiding in Christ, filled with His Spirit, and seeking to be about our Father's business, the Lord is working through us even when we can't detect much observable success. We walk by faith and we work by faith, knowing our labor in the Lord is not in vain. The accumulated results of our labor will compound only after we're gone, and the reverberations will reach all the way to heaven's shoreline.

Compounding with Interest

My friend Jane Meyer gave me a book written by her late husband, Paul Meyer, a successful businessman and motivational expert. Paul got into business as a boy, after asking his dad for a bicycle. Instead of buying one for him, Paul's dad took him to the junkyard where they selected several old bikes. In their garage, Paul disassembled the discarded bicycles and reassembled them into one new version for himself. "With this new knowledge," Paul wrote, "I suddenly found myself with a business opportunity. As a teenager I refurbished and sold over 300 bicycles!"[10]

Paul went on to start more than a hundred companies. He confesses that 65 percent of them have not survived, but even those weren't failures. They were temporary setbacks providing the experience and knowledge needed for future attempts. The companies that *have* been successful have been *very* successful, and, since everything Paul did was utterly dedicated to the Lord Jesus Christ, they have been a source of ministry, have touched millions of people, and have funded hundreds of causes.[11]

Everything can be traced back to a dad who did one thing for his kid—he took him to a junkyard to look for a bicycle. "Whatever it is that God has given us," wrote Meyer, "His desire is that we use it wisely so it multiplies." But he also warns,

> Multiplication may take longer than you planned. There once was a university in England partially enclosed by a

stone wall. An ivy bush was planted beside the wall with hopes that the vines would grow and cover the wall, but after many years, the ivy appeared dormant. Tired of waiting, the groundskeeper decided to give it one more year to grow.

The following year, the ivy began to spread rapidly over the wall. Out of curiosity, he gently dug around the plant and discovered one primary root that went directly toward a river located more than seventy feet away. All those years the ivy bush had been putting its entire effort into reaching the river. Once that was accomplished, multiplication took place at an alarming rate. Had the groundskeeper given up too quickly, multiplication would never have been realized. Delay is part of the multiplication process. It takes time to get everything lined up, but once that occurs, watch out because things are about to erupt.[12] .

Last week a man approached me at the end of our Sunday church services. "I just wanted to tell you I'm here," he said, "because you visited my house ten years ago. You drove up, came to the door, and handed me some literature. I may not have appeared too friendly at the time," he said, "but I've been thinking about it ever since then. So here I am—ten years later."

If you think ten years is a long time to wait for results, let me tell you about John Flavel, a seventeenth-century English Presbyterian preacher. On one occasion, he preached a sermon from 1 Corinthians 16:22: "If any man love not the Lord Jesus Christ, let him be Anathema. Maranatha."[13] The word *anathema* means "cursed." The term *maranatha* means "Come, Lord!" Flavel explained those words in somber tones, and as he concluded the service and prepared to pronounce a blessing, he paused, deeply moved, and said, "How shall I bless this whole assembly, when every person in it who loveth not the Lord Jesus Christ is Anathema?"[14]

Sitting in the service that day was a fifteen-year-old boy named Luke Short, a native of Dartmouth. He heard those words but they had no effect on him. He grew up, immigrated to America, and spent the rest of his life farming. When he was a hundred years old, he still had enough strength to walk across his farm and do his work. His mind was as sharp as a tack. One day in his centennial year as he sat resting in his fields, he reflected over his many days, and he could still hear the voice of John Flavel, long dead, ringing in his ears. He fell under the conviction of the Holy Spirit and gloriously gave his life to Christ—because of a message preached eighty-five years before. Luke Short was misnamed; he was long-lived. He reached his 116th year, full of piety, spiritual fervor, and a love for Jesus and good works.[15]

Here's the conclusion of the whole matter: God has placed you on earth for a special set of tasks, which He has prepared in advance for you to do. Whatever our vocation or status in life, true fulfillment is found when we determine to be about our Father's business, wherever we are, today. As we redeem the time and seek to seize every opportunity, as we organize our lives for effectiveness and maximize the mornings for efficiency, as we take heed to ourselves, strengthen ourselves in the Lord, as we live by faith and relish the joy of the Lord, as we persevere and plod until we can say "I have finished the work." When we truly view our life spans in this way, it repels discouragement.

Scripture assures us the Lord does His work through us whether the tasks are big or little, whether the audience is large or small, whether the recognition comes or not, whether the results seem abundant or meager. Somehow, as we add one day to the next and accomplish one task after another, He gives the plus sign a quarter turn, and all remaining history will multiply the legacy of our lives. Every deed will compound with the ages, and every word will exponentially increase until, at the dawning of eternity, we'll discover what the Bible writers called "a harvest of righteousness" that far exceeds anything we could ask or imagine (James 3:18; Hebrews 12:11; 2 Corinthians 9:10). When we crunch the numbers in heaven, we'll see they had a way of compounding with interest until the exponential results can only be calculated by the angelic book-keepers.

"I planted the seed, Apollos watered it, but God has been making it grow."

—1 Corinthians 3:6

O use me, Lord, use even me,
Just as Thou wilt, and when, and where,
Until Thy blessed face I see,
Thy rest, Thy joy, Thy glory share.

—Frances Ridley Havergal, in her hymn "Lord, Speak to Me"[1]

26

Pipelines of Grace

I want to end this book with a story for anyone who feels it's too late to master life. Perhaps you've tried and failed too many times. Maybe you've stumbled, fallen, and, in discouragement, decided to lie in the leaves rather than rediscover the path. But Proverbs 24:16 says, "No matter how many times you trip them up, God-loyal people don't stay down long."[2]

Last fall, I took my staff to my rural home in Roan Mountain, Tennessee, for our annual retreat. One afternoon while they were working in individual planning sessions, I decided to hike up the mountain behind our house. I chose a different route than usual. All the trails on the mountain are nostalgic for me, because I remember hiking them a half century ago with my father, John I. Morgan, who inherited the land from his father and who passed it on to me. The mountain hollows and hillsides are steep, thickly forested, and dotted with underground springs.

My dad's hobby was locating and tending these springs. I remember hiking with him into the hills many times and watching him locate the springheads of little brooks, which were sometimes nothing more than a marshy spot on the mountainside. He would dynamite and dig into a crevice, isolate a clean source for the water, and build a simple cistern around it with a sort of faucet or aperture, to which he connected black plastic pipe. He unspooled miles and miles of this black plastic pipe, which crisscrossed the mountain from his springs to the reservoir above the house. For many years, that was our water supply. After he and my mom passed away and I moved five hours away, I found it impossible to maintain the springs, and we reluctantly switched to city water. But to this day, whenever I'm hiking through those mountains, I almost always find lengths of his black plastic pipe beneath the thickened layers of leaves and fallen limbs on the forest floor.

Well, on this day I hiked to the top of the mountain by a circuitous route, and it took longer than expected. Reaching a spot I call Pinnacle Rock, I knelt down and prayed for the manuscript of this particular book, which I was starting to piece together. On the return trip, I decided to take a shortcut down the mountain. It was quite steep, and I got myself into a laurel thicket that was so dense I could hardly penetrate it. It covered about an acre. I got so tangled up in the laurel, I wondered if I could get out of it. I was crawling on my stomach and climbing over branches like a child in a jungle gym. I also began worrying about upsetting a bear, knowing the thicket was a perfect home for a mother and her cubs.

Eventually I spied a huge tree that had fallen over a wide swath of the thicket, and it made a bridge. I thought to myself, *If I can just get on that log, I can tightrope over the entire mess.* So I hoisted myself onto the log and began my trek to the other side. But the log was wet and moss-covered and slippery, and when I was halfway across it, my feet flew into thin air. I fell backward about five feet and landed on my back in the one spot where there was no laurel to break my fall. I hit the ground with a thud.

My first instinct was to panic. No one would ever find me in the middle of that thicket, and my cell phone wasn't working. But a quick assessment told me that no bones were broken; and though I was badly jarred, I was able to pull myself to my feet. I looked around, trying to get my bearings, but I was disoriented and couldn't tell east from west. At that moment I looked down, and there right by my feet was one of my dad's black plastic pipes, one he had laid many years ago, one I could follow down the mountain to the reservoir just above our house. I followed the pipe and, limping a bit, made my way back home just in time to shower and show up, looking a little worse for wear, at supper.

I know what it's like to take a tumble so bad you'd rather lie on the forest floor than rediscover the path. But it's always too soon to quit. Maybe you've had a terrible fall. Perhaps you've made a mistake. Maybe you've fallen into a sin. Maybe your plans have fallen apart like a cheap contraption. Perhaps a sense of frustration or failure haunts you, even a sense of futility, and it's kept you from mastering life.

But the Lord Jesus Christ was lifted up and crucified to provide all the forgiveness you need. If you'll pick yourself up right now and determine to make the best use of the path ahead, you'll find that the heavenly Father has a pipeline of grace running right by your footsteps. Psalm 87:7 says, "All my springs are in you."[3]

Your God has gone before you to provide all your needs. He can recalibrate His plans for your life, recalculate your path, and help you begin right now. You can turn trials into trails; you can still master life before it's too late. You can be a pleasant and productive soul, and He can work in your life in ways greater than you can image.

If you'll give everything to Him, He will lead you to the reservoirs of His strength. If you follow the pipelines of His grace, they will lead you home.

Study Questions for Mastering This Pattern

1. What did Charles Spurgeon mean when he said to David Livingstone, "You have forgotten that there are two of us"?

_____

_____

_____

_____

2. What insights most impressed you from Jesus' teaching about the vine and the branches in John 15?

_____

_____

_____

3. According to Ephesians 5:18–21, what are the results or evidences of being filled with the Holy Spirit?

_____

_____

_____

4. Can you think of someone you can encourage with this material? What aspect of this section of _Mastering Life Before It's Too Late_ was most uplifting to you?

_____

_____

_____

_____

For more help in applying these principles or for group study or staff training, download my free _Mastering Life Workbook_ at RobertJMorgan.com/MasteringLifeWorkbook.

ACKNOWLEDGMENTS

In working on this book I've received masterful help from special friends.

Jonathan Merkh and Philis Boultinghouse of Howard Books

Sealy Yates of Yates and Yates

Joshua Rowe and Stephen Fox of Clearly Media

Sherry Anderson of The Donelson Fellowship

Casey Pontioos, who tackled the endnotes

and most of all . . .

Katrina!

NOTES

Introduction: Mastering Life the Master's Way

1 Quoted in the *Friends' Intelligencer and Journal*, 57 (Philadelphia: Society of Friends, October 20, 1900): 773.

2 The Living Bible.

3 This NIV quotation is from the 1984 edition.

4 Quoted by David Bentley-Taylor in *My Dear Erasmus* (London: Christian Focus Publications, 2002), 67.

5 Philip Doddridge, *The Works of the Rev. P. Doddridge, D.D.*, VI (Leeds: Edward Baines, 1804), 338.

1. First Words, Last Words—Our Stencil for Success

1 Quoted in a review of *Osler's Essays* in *Northwest Medicine: Volume VI* (Portland, OR: Northwest Medical Publishing Association, 1914), 187.

2 Psalm 8:2.

3 The New Living Translation.

4 The New King James Translation.

5 For more on the prophetic significance of the twelve-year-old Jesus' experience and teachings, see my book of daily devotions, *All to Jesus* (Nashville: B&H Publishers, 2012), entry for Day 239.

2. Just for Today

1 From the hymn "Lead, Kindly Light," written in 1833 by John Henry Newman.

2 Contemporary English Version.

3 Katharine Fry, *A Memoir of Elizabeth Fry* (London: James Nisbet and Co., 1868), 316.

4 J. Oswald Sanders, *A Spiritual Clinic* (Chicago: Moody Press, 1958), 169.

5 Anna Warner, "One More Day's Work for Jesus," published in *Wayfaring Hymns*, 1869. I tell the story behind his hymn in my book on the Warner sisters, *Jesus Loves Me* (Nashville: Thomas Nelson, 2006).

6 Ibid.

7 Ira Sankey, *My Life and the Story of the Gospel Hymns* (Philadelphia: P. W. Ziegler Co., 1907), 240.

8 Eugene H. Peterson, *A Long Obedience in the Same Direction* (Downers Grove, IL, 2000).

9 J. C. Ryle, *Practical Religion: Being Plain Papers on the Daily Duties, Experience, Danger, and Privileges of Professing Christians* (London: William Hunt and Company, 1887), excerpted from Ryle's essay about zeal. I slightly condensed the segment and updated the punctuation.

10 The Living Bible.

11 The New King James Version.

12 Holman Christian Standard Bible.

13 The American Optometric Association, http://www.aoa.org/patients-and-public/eye-and-vision-problems/glossary-of-eye-and-vision-conditions/myopia?sso=y.

14 *Emerson in his Journals,* selected and edited by Joel Porte (Cambridge, MA: The President and Fellows of Harvard College, 1982), entry for January 26, 1844, p. 320.

15 Andrew Murray, *Abide in Christ* (London: James Nisbet & Co., 1882), 102.

16 The New Living Translation.

17 The Message.

18 New King James Version.

19 Charles Haddon Spurgeon, *Spurgeon's Sermons: Fifth Series* (New York: Sheldon and Company, 1859), 59.

20 Emily Huntington Miller, "A Resolve for Every Morning" in *The Christian Advocate* (New York: Eaton & Mains Publishers, 1909), March 4, 1909, 333.

21 John Maxwell, *Today Matters* (New York: Warner Faith, 2004), 15.

22 Ibid., 14, 19.

23 John P. Hopps, from his hymn "Father, Lead Me Day by Day," published in 1877.

24 George Dawson, *Prayers with a Discourse on Prayer* (London: Kegan Paul, Trench & Co., 1882).

3. The Most Pleasant Life Anyone Can Live

1 Frances Ridley Havergal, *My King and His Service* (Philadelphia: Henry Altemus, 1892), 48.

2 Quoted by Martin H. Manser in *The Westminster Collection of Christian Quotes* (Louisville, KY: Westminster John Knox Press, 2001), 35.

3 https://www.goodreads.com/quotes/860733-it-s-not-enough-to-be-busy-so-are-the-ants.

4 The New King James Version.

5 J. Oswald Sanders, *A Spiritual Clinic* (Chicago: Moody Press, 1958), 160.

6 The Good News Translation.

7 The Message.

8 See, for example, Winnie Hu, "In a New Generation of College Students, Many Opt for the Life Examined, " *The New York Times,* April 2, 2008.

9 Paul Strathern, *Bertrand Russell in 90 Minutes* (Chicago: Ivan R. Dee, 2001), 12.

10 Ibid., 15.

11 Ibid., 17.

12 Bertrand Russell, *Autobiography* (London: Routledge, 1998), 194.

13 Richard Baxter, *The Practical Works of Richard Baxter* (London: James Duncan, 1830), Vol. 3, 130.

14 *Choice Sayings of Dying Saints* (Edinburgh: William Oliphant and Company, 1866), 46. Author/Editor anonymous.

15 Joseph Conder, in his hymn "Day by Day the Manna Fell," published in 1836.

4. Life Is Just a Minute

1 This poem appeared unattributed in *The Educator-Journal*, Vol. XV, no. 1, published in Indianapolis (Sept. 1914): 188. It has been quoted many times, including by Robert Schuller, who states that he worked with Dr. Mays and heard him often say these words. Schuller included the poem in his book *Power Thoughts: Achieve Your True Potential through Power Thinking* (New York: HarperCollins, 1993), 115.

2 Billy Graham, *Just As I Am* (New York: HarperCollins, 1997), 720.

3 Quoted on multiple internet sites.

4 J. H. Jewett, "The Watchful Use of Opportunity," in *Moody Bible Institute Monthly, Volume 22*, January 1922, 778.

5 Quoted in *Orations and Speeches on Various Occasions*, II, compiled by Edward Everett (Boston: Charles C. Little and James Brown, 1850), 562.

6 The second hand made its first appearance on a clock in 1680, but in America clock-making was expensive and time-consuming, and most clocks were kept as simple as possible. See Warman's *American Clocks Field Guide* (Iola, WI: Krause Publications, 2003), 7.

7 This is common knowledge, and this information is on most websites and articles connected with the story of clocks and watches. Many watchmakers have a page on their websites devoted to the history of their timepieces. Wristwatches were in existence prior to the 1920s, but only after World War I did they become popular. See, for example, the Elgin explanation at http://elginpocketwatch .net/elgin-pocket-watch-cases-explained/.

8 *Look* magazine, March 5, 1957.

5. The Bible's Twin Texts on Time

1 Quoted in *Treasury of Wisdom, Wit and Humor, Odd Compari-*

sons and Proverbs, compiled by Adam Woolever (Philadelphia: E. Claxton & Company, 1881), 372–73.

2 *The Voice of Wisdom, A Treasury of Moral Truths,* edited by J.E. (Edinburgh: William P. Nimmo & Co, 1883), 33

3 *Time's Telescope for 1830* (London: Sherwood, Gilbert, and Piper, 1830), 4.

4 A. W. Tozer used this phrase in his book *The Knowledge of the Holy* (New York: Harper & Brothers, 1961), chapter 7.

5 The Message.

6 John Milton, *The Poems of John Milton* (New York: P. F. Collier & Con Company, 1909), 356.

7 Samuel Smiles, *Self-Help* (New York: American Book Company, 1904), 163.

8 Benjamin Franklin, *The Works of Benjamin Franklin, Volume IV* (Philadelphia: William Duane, 1809), 237.

9 English Standard Version.

10 For example, the King James Version, among others.

11 For example, the New International Version, among others.

12 The Voice.

13 Alexander Kelly McClure, *Abe Lincoln's Yarns and Stories* (New York: Western W. Wilson, 1901), 385. Lincoln's exact quote was: "I feel like a man letting lodgings at one end of the house while the other end is on fire."

14 Widely quoted. See for example, *Human Resource Management: Third Edition* (New Delhi: Excell Books, 2010), Appendix 11:2, 320.

15 Samuel Logan Brengle, *The Soul Winner's Secret* (London: The Salvation Army Publishing Department, 1903): 31.

6. Living Clockwise

1 Andrew Murray, *Abide in Christ* (London: James Nisbet & Co., 1882), 99.

2 This is widely quoted but I have yet to find it footnoted or attributed.

3 Eugene H. Peterson, *The Contemplative Pastor* (Grand Rapids: Eerdmans, 1989), 17–18.

4   Cal Newport in *Manage Your Day-To-Day,* Jocelyn K. Glei, ed. (Las Vegas: Amazon Publishing, 2013), 73.

5   Everyone should read Hummel's little booklet, published by InterVarsity, which circulated widely on the Christian campus I attended and was a help to all who read it.

6   Many groups have jumped onto the 30/30 bandwagon, including: Running expert Hal Higdon and the 30/30 plan for runners, at http://www.halhigdon.com/training/51237/rr/Beginning-Runners-Guide-30-30-Plan; the 30/30 plan for improving employee proficiency developed by Learning Paths International at http://www.learningpathsinternational.com/30-30plan.html; the 30/30 plan for teaching kids about disaster awareness at http://www.floridadisaster.org/kids/downloads/Grade1_30-30Rule.pdf. There is a popular study philosophy called the 30-30 schedule that advocates intense focus on an assignment for 30 minutes, followed by 30 minutes of leisure; for example, at http://www.textfugu.com/season-3/finding-time/1-2/. The popularity of these plans points to the simplicity and importance of reclaiming control over even brief segments of time for a sustained period.

7   New King James Version.

8   Robert J. Morgan, *The Red Sea Rules* (Nashville: Thomas Nelson Publishers, 2001), chapter 6.

9   Quoted by William Swinton in *Sixth or Classic English Reader* (New York: American Book Company, 1885), 422.

7. Gather the Fragments That Remain

1   *Thoughts,* complied by the Ladies of Fabiola Hospital Association, Oakland California (New York: Dodge Publishing Company, 1918), 92.

2   Quoted in *The Speaker's Quote Book,* edited by Roy B. Zuck (Grand Rapids: Kregel Publications, 1997), 417.

3   Lord Byron, from his poem, "Don Juan" in *The Words of Lord Byron: Including the Suppressed Poems, Complete in One Volume* (Paris: A. and W. Galignani, 1828), 599.

4   New King James Version.

5   J. Oswald Sanders, *A Spiritual Clinic* (Chicago: Moody Press, 1958), 166.

6   http://www.brainyquote.com/quotes/quotes/c/charles-cal108128.html.

7   Henry David Thoreau, *Walden* (New York: Thomas Y. Crowell and Company, 1910), 8.

8   J. Oswald Sanders, *A Spiritual Clinic* (Chicago: Moody Press, 1958), 166–67.

9   Reagan mentions this several times, among other places in Ronald Reagan, *The Reagan Diaries*, Douglas Brinkley, ed. (New York: HarperCollins, 2007). See, for example, pages 48, 560, 677.

10   I previously related this story in my book on Scripture memory, *100 Verses Everyone Should Know By Heart* (Nashville: B&H Publishers, 2010).

8. God Is Not Disorganized—Why Are You?

1   Samuel Logan Brengle, *The Soul Winners Secret* (London: The Salvation Army Publishing Department, 1903), 31. Brengle's chapter about the usage of time is the best advice I've ever read on the subject.

2   Jim Furgerson, Pastor, Tilden Baptist Church, 15339 Spring Rock, San Antonio, Texas, 78247. jfurg@sbcglobal.net.

3   "Decluttering Before the New Year" by Maureen Jenkins, at www.cnn.com/2012/12/26/living/declutter-before-new-year/.

4   The Living Bible.

5   Mark 6:40 and John 6:12.

6   John 20:6–8, The Message.

7   1 Corinthians 14:33 and 40, NASV.

8   The Message.

9   God's Word Translation.

10   The Message.

11   God's Word Translation.

12   The Living Bible.

13   Good News Translation.

14   The Message.

15   Ibid.

16 Ibid.

17 Ibid.

18 A. W. Tozer, *A Treasury of A. W. Tozer* (Grand Rapids: Baker, 1980), 233.

19 http://www.breitbart.com/Big-Peace/2014/05/26/Commencement-Address-by-Admiral-William-McRaven.

9. Put Your Tray Tables in Their Upright Positions

1 George Dawson, *Prayer with a Discourse on Prayer* (London: Kegan Paul, Trench & Co, 1882), 91.

2 Henry David Thoreau, *Walden* (New York: Barnes & Noble Books, 2004), 29.

3 Ibid., 77–78.

4 Sunbeams: A Book of Quotations, edited by Sy Safransky (Berkley, CA: North Atlantic Books, 1990), 44. Also see http://en.wikiquote.org/wiki/Gustave_Flaubert.

5 http://www.brainyquote.com/quotes/quotes/n/napo leonbo140390.html

6 New Living Translation.

10. Don't Be Listless

1 Charles Dickens, *Words of Charles Dickens: David Copperfield, Volume II* (New York: Hurd and Houghton, 1873), 246.

2 Mason Currey, *Daily Rituals: How Artists Work* (New York: Alfred A. Knopf, 2013), introduction.

3 New Century Version.

4 David Allen, *Getting Things Done: The Art of Stress-Free Productivity* (New York: Penguin Books, 2001), 7.

5 Ibid., 13–14.

6 Ibid., 3.

7 Douglas C. Merrill, *Getting Organized in the Google Era* (New York: Broadway Books, 2010), 8.

8 Tom Clancy, *Debt of Honor* (New York: Berkley, 1994), 581.

11. Awake, My Soul, and with the Sun

1   Quoted by Charles Noel Douglas in *Forty Thousand Sublime and Beautiful Thoughts* (New York: The Christian Herald, 1915), 1196.

2   For more information about the history of hymns, see my three-volume set of books, *Then Sings My Soul.*

3   Samuel Logan Brengle, *The Soul Winner's Secret* (London: The Salvation Army Publishing Department, 1903), 29.

4   From the *Katholisches Gesangbuch* (Würzburg, Germany: c. 1744) (*Beim frühen Morgenlicht*); translated from German to English by Edward Caswall in Formby's *Catholic Hymns* (London: 1854).

12. Our First Appointment Each Day

1   *The Practice of the Presence of God* is the title of a much-loved Christian classic by Father Joseph de Beaufort, based on the teachings of Nicholas Herman, otherwise known as Brother Lawrence, and published after Herman's death in 1601.

2   Quoted in *The Missionary Review of the World,* Rev. Arthur T. Pierson, ed. (New York: Funk & Wagnalls, 1905), 652.

3   Stephen Charnock, *Discourses on the Existence and Attributes of God* (New York: RT Carter & Brother, 1874), 310–11. I previously wrote this paraphrased version of Charnock's sentences as part of the introduction to *The Unchanging Word,* published by Turning Point Ministries in 2013.

4   For more information about Scripture memory, check out my book *100 Bible Verses Everyone Should Know By Heart.*

5   I write more extensively about the techniques of a daily Quiet Time in my book *SIMPLE: The Christian Life Doesn't Have to be Complicated* (Nashville: Randall House Publications, 2008). The following three illustrations from Bertha Smith, Thomas Watson, and Iris Clinton, are repeated from chapter 6 of that book.

6   Bertha Smith, *Go Home and Tell* (Nashville: Broadman & Holman, 1995), 76.

7   Iris Clinton, *Young Man in a Hurry: The Story of William Carey*

(Fort Washington, PA: Christian Literature Crusade, 1961), 55–56.

8 Thomas Watson, *Gleanings from Thomas Watson* (Morgan, PA: Soli Deo Gloria Publications, 1995, first published in London in 1915), 107.

9 George Muller, *The Life of Trust: Being a Narrative of the Lord's Dealings with George Muller* (Boston: Gould and Lincoln, 1868), 206–7.

13. Before Leaving the Presence

1 Hugh Blair, *Sermons* (Philadelphia: Hickman & Hazzard, 1822), 195.

2 Brian Tracy, *Eat That Frog* (San Francisco: Berrett-Koehler Publishers, 2008), 8.

3 Ibid., 108.

4 Ibid., 130.

5 This story is found many places, including R. Alec Mackenzie, *The Time Trap* (New York: McGraw-Hill, 1972), 38–39.

6 Ibid.

7 Andrew Murray, *Abide in Christ* (London: James Nisbet & Co., 1882), 103.

14. Try the Fifteen-Minute Plan

1 Oswald Chambers, *My Utmost for His Highest* (Oswald Chambers Publications Association, Ltd), installment for August 23.

15. Make Wise Withdrawals

1 The Living Bible.

2 Quoted in *Praise: Webster's Quotations, Facts, and Phrases* (San Diego: ICON Group International, 2008), 3.

3 Mrs. Charles E. Cowman in *Springs in the Valley* (Los Angeles: Cowman Publications, Inc., 1939), 218.

4 "The Most Important Thing You Can Do in the New Year to Lose Weight, Get Sharper and Live Longer" in the *Huffington Post*, January 1, 2014, at http://www.huffingtonpost.com

/2013/12/29/sleep-health-benefits_n_4461303.html?utm
_hp_ref=healthy-living.

16. Take Heed to Yourself

1   A Selection from the Spiritual Letters of S. Francis de Sales, H. L. Sidney Lear, ed. (New York: E. P. Dutton, 1876), 228.
2   Quoted by J. Oswald Chambers in *Spiritual Leadership* (Chicago: Moody, 1967), 109.
3   New King James Version.
4   Psalm 37:3, 5, 6, New King James Version.
5   Roy King, *Time Management Is Really Life Management* (Columbia, SC: LeaderSpace, 2009), 30.
6   J. Oswald Sanders, *A Spiritual Clinic* (Chicago: Moody Press, 1958), 170.
7   "Take Time to Be Holy" by William Longstaff, 1882.

17. Only Do What Only You Can Do

1   Vance Havner, *Peace in the Valley* (Grand Rapids: Fleming H. Revell Company, 1962), 30.
2   Quoted by Jesse Irvine Overholtzer in a testimony filed in the archives at Child Evangelism Fellowship in a folder entitled "Testimonies of Mr. O."
3   "Involving Children in Household Tasks: Is It Worth the Effort?" at http://www.cehd.umn.edu/research/highlights/Rossmann/.
4   Fred Smith, Sr., *Breakfast with Fred* (Ventura, CA: Regal, 2007), 53.
5   Michael Hyatt on his blog "The Not to Do List" at http://michaelhyatt.com/the-not-to-do-list.html.

18. The Art of Strengthening Yourself in the Lord

1   New King James Version.
2   Dr. Kane's story has been widely discussed in medical books and journals as well as in the popular media. I first came across the story in *More of Paul Harvey's The Rest of the Story* by Paul

Aurandt, edited and complied by Lynee Harvey (New York: William Morrow, 1980), 111–12. Also see, for example, the Wikipedia entry http://en.wikipedia.org/wiki/Evan_O'Neill _Kane; also Lawrence K. Altman, *Who Goes First?: The Story of Self-Experimentation in Medicine* (Berkeley and Los Angeles, CA: University of California Press, 1987), 413.

3   Robert J. Morgan, *100 Bible Verses Everyone Should Know By Heart* (Nashville: B&H Books, 2010), 20.

4   Samuel Clarke, *A Collection of the Sweet Assuring Promises of Scripture* (New York: Lane & Scott, 1848), introduction.

5   William Law, *A Serious Call to a Devout and Holy Life* (Newcastle: J. Barker, 1845), 45.

6   See Isaiah 40:31; Psalm 23:3; Ephesians 3:16–19; Deuteronomy 33:25.

19. Harness the Psychology of the Soul

1   This quotation is widely attributed to William James in newer books and on popular quotation websites, but I haven't been able to give it definite attribution. It may be a summary or paraphrase of James's philosophy.

2   William Shakespeare, *Hamlet, Prince of Denmark*, Act 3, scene 4.

3   Theodore Roosevelt, *Theodore Roosevelt, an Autobiography* (New York: Charles Scribner's Sons, 1922), 52. Italics are mine.

4   Ibid. Italics are mine.

5   William James, "The Gospel of Relaxation" in *Scribner's Magazine* XXV (January–June 1899): 500. Italics are mine.

6   Quoted by Alan Loy McGinnis, *The Power of Optimism* (San Francisco: Harper & Row, 1990), 96. Italics are mine.

7   Lexham English Bible.

8   Robert J. Morgan, *The Promise* (Nashville: B&H Publishers, 2008), 3.

9   Frederick William Faber, from his hymn "I Worship Thee, Most Gracious God," written in 1849 under the original title "I Worship Thee, Sweet Will of God."

10   Father Cuthbert, *The Life of St. Francis of Assisi* (New York: Longmans, Green, and Co., 1925), 419. Italics are mine.

11   New King James Version.

12   Charles Haddon Spurgeon, in his sermon "True Prayer—True Power!" preached on Sunday morning, August 12, 1860, at Exeter Hall, Strand. (Italics mine.) A transcription of the published sermon can be found at http://www.spurgeon.org/sermons/0328.htm.

13   Albert Barnes, *Notes, Explanatory and Practical, on the New Testament: Volume IX—Hebrews* (London: Blackie & Son, n.d.), 249.

14   See C. S. Lewis, *Mere Christianity*, in *The Complete C.S. Lewis Signature Classics* (New York: HarperOne, 2002), 110–11.

15   Dale Carnegie, *How to Stop Worrying and Start Living* (New York: Simon and Schuster, 1948), 202–3.

16   These phrases are from the song "A Spoonful of Sugar," by Robert B. Sherman and Richard M. Sherman, from the 1964 movie musical *Mary Poppins*.

17   Dale Carnegie, *How To Stop Worrying and Start Living* (New York: Simon and Schuster, 1948), 202–3.

18   The book Katrina read was *Enthusiasm Makes the Difference* by Norman Vincent Peale (Englewood Cliffs, NJ: Prentice-Hall, Inc., 1967).

19   Brother Lawrence, *The Practice of the Presence of God* (London: H. R. Allenson, 1906), 26, 28, italics mine.

20   Henry David Thoreau, *Walden* (New York: Barnes & Noble Books, 2004), 343.

20. The Singular Secret of Unsinkable Saints

1   Wilber Fisk Crafts, *Trophies of Song* (Boston: D. Lothrop & Co., 1874), 123.

2   New King James Version.

3   Based on a personal interview between Mr. Tipton and the author and used with permission. You can also find this story in James R. Newby, *Shining Out and Shining In: Understanding the Life Journey of Tom Tipton* (Bloomington, IN: AuthorHouse LLC, 2013), where this story is recounted on pages xix–xx.

4   King James Version.

5   New King James Version.

6   Ibid.

7   See the English Standard Version.

8   Jonathan Edwards, *Selected Sermons of Jonathan Edwards* (New York: The MacMillan Company, 1904), 21.

9   Dr. Lloyd Byers shared this material in a personal interview with the author; used with permission. This material is also found in Dr. Lloyd Byers, *Keep Moving Forward: My Son's Last Words* (Bloomington, IN: WestBow Press, 2011). See especially chapter 9.

10   Based on a personal interview and correspondence; used with permission.

11   Quoted in *The Path to Heaven* (London: Burns, Lambert, and Oaks, undated), 234.

12   John Berridge, *Cheerful Piety; Or, Religion without Gloom* (Brooklyn: Thomas Kirk, 1812).

13   Hannah Whitall Smith, *The Unselfishness of God and How I Discovered It* (London: Fleming H. Revell, 1903), 290, condensed slightly.

21. The Executive Joy of Pleasantly Productive Leadership

1   Quoted in *The Westminster Collection of Christian Quotations*, compiled by Martin H. Manser (Louisville, Kentucky: Westminster John Knox Press), 214.

2   Joseph Addison and Baron Thomas Babington, *Select Essays of Addison*, Samuel Thurber, ed. (Boston: Allyn and Bacon, 1892), 200.

3   *Theological Wordbook of the Old Testament, Volume 2*, compiled by R. Laird Harris, Gleason L. Archer, Jr., and Bruce K. Waltke (Chicago: Moody Bible Institute, 1980), 879.

4   This is widely attributed to Robert Lewis Stevenson. See, for example, Robert Louis Stevenson and Florence Tucker, *Stevenson Day by Day* (New York: Thomas Y. Crowell & Company, 1909), 22.

5   New International Version, 1984.

6   Thomas O. Chisholm, "Great Is Thy Faithfulness," published in 1923.

7   New King James Version.

8   Ibid.

9   Ibid.

10 Ibid.

11 Ibid.

12 Ernest Hemingway, *A Moveable Feast: The Restored Edition* (New York: Scribner, 2009), xii.

13 Quoted in *To America* by Stephen E. Ambrose (New York: Simon & Schuster Paperbacks, 2002), 97.

14 Quoted by John Berridge in *Cheerful Piety; Or, Religion without Gloom* (Brooklyn: Thomas Kirk, 1812), title page.

15 Jay Kesler, *Being Holy, Being Human* (Ada, MI: Bethany House, 1994), 44.

22. Well Versed in Happiness

1   http://www.spurgeon.org/sermons/1027.htm.

2   H. W. Brands, *The First American: The Life and Times of Benjamin Franklin* (NY: Random House, 2000), 300.

3   Robert J. Morgan, *100 Bible Verses Everyone Should Know By Heart* (Nashville: B&H Publishers, 2010), xiii.

4   Emphasis mine in this and subsequent verses in this chapter.

5   New King James Version.

6   Matthew Henry, *Memoir of the Rev. Philip Henry* (New York: American Tract Society), 123.

7   King James Version.

8   The Voice Translation.

9   Quoted by William Thomas Ellis, *Billy Sunday: The Man and His Message* (L. T. Myers, 1914), 221.

10 Quoted by Mary Allette Ayer in *Keep Up Your Courage* (Boston: Lothrop, Lee & Shepard Co, 1908), 161.

23. Don't Despise the Day of Small Things

1   John Oxenham, *Bees in Amber* (New York: American Tract Society, 1913), 121.

2   Anthony Trollope, *An Autobiography,* vol. 1 (Edinburgh: William Blackwood and Sons, 1883), 160–61.

3   New King James Version.

4   Quoted by Jan Karon in *A Continual Feast* (New York: Viking Press, 2005), unnumbered page.

5   Quoted by Mary W. Tileston in *Daily Strength for Daily Needs* (Boston: Little, Brown, and Company, 1913), 47 (entry for February 16).

6   Mary Drewery, *William Carey: A Biography* (Grand Rapids: Zondervan, 1978), 90. The list of Carey's accomplishments was collected from a biography or biographies that are no longer in my possession, but the facts are well documented. Any duplication of phraseology is unintentional.

7   Eustace Carey, *Memoir of William Carey, D.D.* (Jackson & Walford, 1836), 623. The quotes from his brother and sister are also found in Eustace Carey's *Memoir*, 24, 39, 623.

8   See any dictionary that includes etymologies, or online dictionary sites such as https://www.wordnik.com/words/plod.

9   I'm indebted to Warren W. Wiersbe for this Spurgeon quote and for his insights on plodding, found in his book *In Praise of Plodders* (Grand Rapids: Kregel Resources, 1994), 11–12.

10 Robert J. Morgan, *All to Jesus* (Nashville: B&H Publishers, 2012), Devotion 259.

11 Dante Alighieri, *La Divina Commedia*, Vol. 3 (N. Carli, 1813), 37.

24. Double Vision

1   The Message.

2   This story is adapted from numerous sources including Paul Aurandt, *More of Paul Harvey's The Rest of the Story* (New York: William Morrow and Company, Inc., 1980), 76–77; in John C. Maxwell's *Power of Partnership in the Church* (Nashville: J. Countryman, 1999), 109; and in *Good Housekeeping*, vol. 191. Any duplication of phrases is unintentional, as I sought to draw on various sources.

3   Russell Herman Conwell, *Life of Charles Haddon Spurgeon* (Edgewood Publishing Company, 1892), 235.

4   Verses 4–6; English Standard Version.

5   To learn more about Hudson Taylor's discovery, see *Hudson*

Taylor's Spiritual Secret by Dr. and Mrs. Howard Taylor (Chicago: Moody Press), 1955.

6   From the hymn "Have Thine Own Way," by Adelaide A. Pollard, published in 1907.

7   Major W. Ian Thomas, *The Saving Life of Christ* (Grand Rapids: Zondervan, 1961), 9.

8   This story is told by Dr. Gordon in *The Northfield Year-Book for Each New Day,* edited by Delavan Leonard Pierson (New York: Fleming H. Revell Company, 1896), 152.

9   John 7:37–39.

25. God's Arithmetic

1   Various models of this experiment vary due to varying thicknesses of the hypothetical sheets of paper.

2   Many engineers have devoted spare moments to the paper-folding hypotheses. See, for example: Camilla De la Bédoyère, *The Science of a Piece of Paper* (Pleasantville, NY: Gareth Stevens Publishing, 2009), 8–9; Clifford A. Pickover, *The Math Book* (New York: Sterling Publishing Company, 2009), 504; and many other such books and journals, along with a variety of websites devoted to this hypothetical exercise, such as http://scienceblogs.com /startswithabang/2009/08/31/paper-folding-to-the-moon/. The calculations of each source may vary slightly, but all report essentially the same set of results.

3   I first came across the story of John Sung in Ruth Tucker's book, *Stories of Faith* (Grand Rapids: Zondervan, 1989), 20. Also see John T. Seamands, *Pioneers of the Younger Churches* (Nashville: Abingdon, 1967) and Leslie T. Lyall, *A Biography of John Sung* (Singapore: Armour Publishing, 2004), especially pages 40–41. Additional information is available on the Wikipedia entry for John Sung Shang Chieh and at a variety of other websites.

4   Stanley Barnes, *A Pictorial History of the 1859 Revival and Related Awakenings in Ulster* (Belfast: Ambassador Publications, 2008), 64–65. As an added note, my alma mater, Columbia International University, where I first became acquainted with

many of the principles in this book, was started by Dr. Robert C. McQuilkin. I asked his son, Dr. Robertson McQuilkin, who succeed him, if there was a connection to the James McQuilkin of the Irish Revival, but such a connection has not yet been determined with certainty.

5   New King James Version.

6   New King James Version.

7   John Woodbridge, *More Than Conquerors* (Chicago: Moody, 1992), 131–33.

8   Ibid.

9   Some of the material in this chapter was first produced in conjunction with Dr. David Jeremiah and *Turning Points* magazine in an article titled "People By the Numbers," for the January 2013 issue of *Turing Points*.

10   Paul J. Meyer, *24 Keys That Bring Complete Success* (Orlando: Bridge-Logos, 2006), 26–27.

11   Ibid.

12   Ibid., 91–94.

13   King James Version.

14   Thomas Jackson, *Curiosities of the Pulpit* (New York: Virtue and Yorston Publishers, 1868), 153–54.

15   Ibid.

26. Pipelines of Grace

1   Frances Ridley Havergal, from her poem, "Lord, Speak to Me," written in 1872.

2   The Message.

3   New King James Version.